W9-COA-777

This book belongs to: ....

My Day

My Day
by
Victoria Roberts

CHATTO & WINDUS · THE HOGARTH PRESS LONDON

Published in 1984 by
Chatto & Windus · The Hogarth Press
40 William IV Street
London WC2N 4DF

All rights reserved. No part of this publication may be reproduced,
stored in a retrieval system, or transmitted in any form, or by any
means, electronic, mechanical, photocopying, recording or otherwise,
without the prior permission of the publisher.

Roberts, Victoria
My day
1. Australian wit and humour, Pictorial
I. Title
741.5'994   NC 1756
ISBN 0 7011 2885 2

Copyright © Victoria Roberts, 1984

Printed in Great Britain by
Butler & Tanner Ltd, Frome and London

For Ma, Mimita, the Holey Family and the Three Kings.

VR

Acknowledgments
I can never do anything alone. Without the
encouraging nods and prods from Mike Morris,
Kevin Gallagher, Sandra Alexander and
Michele Field, I expect I would still be in my
basement, tending to cacti, no book behind me.
But occasionally you need a cup of tea. Thanks
to Ethel O'Brien, who so kindly provided 1078
cups with milk/without sugar for me over the
past year.
And Mum. And Mimita.
And Tom T. and Betty B. who lent me all of
their biographies and still think I am going to
return them.
And Helen Bayliss, librarian extraordinaire,
who has been so very generous in helping me
with the research for this book.
V.R.

My Day by Woody Allen

7 A.M. - I AWAKEN AFTER A HORRIFIC NIGHTMARE. I AM DEAD AND THERE ARE NO BURIAL SITES LEFT IN NEW YORK, SO MY AGENT SENDS MY BODY TO CALIFORNIA.

I TRY TO COMB MY HAIR, BUT I AM A HAIRLESS CASE (DIANE DIDN'T MIND MY HAIR).

I CONSOLE MYSELF WITH AN EXOTIC BREAKFAST IN-STEAD... (SHE CERTAINLY LOVED SHELLFISH).

BUT I AM RUDELY INTERRUP-TED BY MY NEIGHBORS PLAYING WAGNER. I AM NOT FOND OF WAGNER.

MY MOTHER KNOWS HOW I HATE WAGNER, MY ANA-LYST KNOWS HOW I HATE WAGNER, EVEN MY NEIGH-BORS KNOW HOW I HATE WAGNER.

I TRY TO DISTRACT MYSELF WITH MY ALPHABET BLOCKS. I MIGHT CALL DIANE.

I CALL DIANE.

SHE IS HAVING DINNER WITH PAUL SIMON. I TAKE A WALK.

NEXT WEEK SHE'LL BE BRUNCHING WITH ADOLF HITLER.

I TRY TO TAKE A NAP, BUT I KEEP GETTING VIDEOTAPE REPLAYS OF MY CALIFORNIA FUNERAL WITH CANNED SOBS.

BY NOW PAUL IS TELLING DIANE HOW HE WISHES HE WERE A KELLOG'S CORNFLAKE NO DOUBT.

I GUESS MY ANALYST IS RIGHT. I NEED A MAGI-CIAN, NOT AN ANALYST.

My Day by Francis Bacon

SOMETIME A.M. - I AWAKEN, TO FIND MY EMOTIONAL LIFE IS IN THE WAY.

BUT I TRANSCEND IT,

AND SETTLE DOWN TO POPE I;

THEN TO POPES II THRU V.

I DESTROY POPES I AND II, A WISE MOVE SINCE VELASQUEZ PAINTED THIS PAINTING PERFECTLY IN THE SEVENTEENTH CENTURY.

LUNCHTIME - I DECIDE TO BUY SOME VEGETABLES FOR SOUP, BUT I AM DISTRACTED.

STILL DISTRACTED, I VISIT THE LOCAL CHURCH. I FEEL LIKE VISITING THE SISTINE CHAPEL, BUT WHEN NOT IN ROME...

I AM FEELING BETTER. I FIND A LOVELY BOOK WITH HAND-COLOURED PLATES OF DISEASES OF THE MOUTH IN A SECOND HAND SHOP. I'VE ALWAYS HOPED TO PAINT THE MOUTH LIKE MONET PAINTED THE SUNSET.

PEOPLE AROUND ME HAVE BEEN DYING LIKE FLIES— I'VE GOT NOBODY LEFT TO PAINT. I TRY A SELF-PORTRAIT.

GOSH. I HAVE ONE FRIEND LEFT! I'D FORGOTTEN! (AND VERY GOOD LOOKING TOO.) I GIVE UP SELF-PORTRAITS.

I'VE ALWAYS THOUGHT OF FRIENDSHIP AS WHERE TWO PEOPLE TEAR ONE ANOTHER APART AND PERHAPS LEARN SOMETHING FROM ONE ANOTHER. IT'S JUST LIKE THAT!

I THINK ABOUT TEXTURE (TOO MUCH). I DREAM THAT THE SPHINX AND OTHER LARGE EGYPTIAN THINGS ARE MADE OF BUBBLE GUM. I'LL GET MY NERVE ENDINGS ON CANVAS.... TOMORROW.

My Day by Ernest Hemingway

5:47 A.M. I RISE. THE SUN ALSO RISES. BECAUSE MY EYELIDS ARE ESPECIALLY THIN AND EYES EXTREMELY SENSITIVE TO LIGHT I HAVE SEEN ALL THE SUNRISES THERE HAVE BEEN IN MY LIFE.

MY MIND STARTS MAKING SENTENCES. I TAKE MY PILLS AND JUMP INTO THE RING. THE FIRST ROUND IS A CINCH: DIALOGUE—WHEN PEOPLE ARE TALKING I CAN HARDLY WRITE IT FAST ENOUGH.

I USE THE OLDEST WORDS IN THE ENGLISH LANGUAGE. PEOPLE THINK I'M AN IGNORANT BASTARD WHO DOESN'T KNOW THE TEN DOLLAR WORDS. I KNOW THE TEN DOLLAR WORDS.

I STARTED OUT VERY QUIET AND I BEAT MR. TURGENEV. THEN I TRAINED HARD AND BEAT MR. DE MAUPASSANT.

MRS. HEMINGWAY SAYS I SHOULD GET A MOVE ON AND COME DOWN TO BREAKFAST. NEVER LEAD AGAINST A HITTER UNLESS YOU CAN OUT HIT HIM.

MRS. H. IS ONE OF THE BEST THAT'S EVER COME INTO THE RING. SHE'S NURSED ME THROUGH ANTHRAX, KIDNEY TROUBLE, PNEUMONIA, A BROKEN ARM. AND MAX EASTMAN'S REVIEW OF "DEATH IN THE AFTERNOON"...

OR WAS THAT ANOTHER MRS. HEMINGWAY? ANYWAY, EASTMAN'S A SWINE, A TRAITOR ALSO IMPOTENT AND JEALOUS AS HELL OF A MAN WHO CAN BEAT TH SH— OUT OF HIM AND WRITE AS WELL.

I FEEL LIKE TALKING. I PHONE SCOTT FITZGERALD AND TELL HIM HOW TO WRITE.

I DON'T WANT TO TALK ANYMORE. I GO FISHING INSTEAD AND REMEMBER ITALY. WE SHOT THREE HUNDRED AND THIRTY ONE DUCKS TO SIX GUNS THERE ONE MORNING.

AND PARIS— THERE WEREN'T ANY ELK, MOOSE, OR BLACK BEARS IN PARIS, BUT THERE WAS GERTRUDE STEIN.

I SHOOT TWELVE LITTLE BIRDS AND TURN IN FOR A "DEATH IN THE AFTERNOON", A COCKTAIL MADE WITH ABSINTHE AND VERMOUTH,

FOLLOWED BY A VERMOUTHLESS MARTINI, TEQUILA, AND BOURBON. ONLY SUCKERS WORRY ABOUT SAVING THEIR SOULS. GOODNIGHT.

My Day by Margaret Thatcher

4:30 A.M. - I AWAKEN. I DO NOT READ THE GUARDIAN

I WRITE A SPEECH INSTEAD ON THAT UN-PALATABLE CONSE-QUENCE OF FIGHTING INFLATION - UNEMPLOYMENT.

I TRY NOT TO REPEAT MYSELF. THE SHORTEST CURRENCY IN THE WORLD, YOU KNOW, IS THE CURRENCY OF NEW IDEAS.

DENNIS, MARK AND I BREAKFAST. MARK COM-PLAINS ABOUT THE IN-STANT COFFEE. I REMIND HIM THAT WE ARE, AFTER ALL, ON PUBLIC SECTOR MONEY.

I SEE TO MY OWN CLOTHES. I CAN'T HELP LOOKING CLEAN. I SHOULD MAKE BBC PERSONALITY OF THE YEAR AGAIN THIS YEAR. I GOT FOUR TIMES AS MA-NY VOTES AS THE QUEEN MOTHER LAST TIME.

I ALWAYS APPRECIATE THE OTHER PERSON'S PRO-BLEM. DEEP IN THEIR INSTINCTS PEOPLE KNOW I'M RIGHT BECAUSE I AM. THAT IS THE WAY I WAS BROUGHT UP.

THE PHONE RINGS. IT IS A CABINET MINISTER WHO DISPLEASES ME. I WITHDRAW MY LOVE. AS PRIME MINISTER I CAN'T WASTE ANY TIME ON INTERNAL ARGUMENTS.

I INSPECT A CIVIL DEPART-MENT INSTEAD. CIVIL SER-VANTS NOT ONLY APPEAR TO BE A DYING BREED, A LARGE PERCENTAGE OF THEM APPEAR TO BE DEAD.

3 P.M. - I TALK TO THE YOUNG UNEMPLOYED ABOUT SKILLS - IF THEY HAVEN'T GOT THEM, THEN THEY HAD BETTER ACQUIRE THEM.

4 P.M. TEA WITH HER MAJESTY. WE'RE BOTH DELIGHTED THAT PRINCE PHILLIP AND DENNIS HAVE HIT IT OFF SO WELL - WEIGHT OFF OUR MINDS, REALLY.

DENNIS MAKES A SHE-PERD'S PIE. HE TELLS ME THE LATEST ON THE NATIONAL SOCIETY FOR THE PROTECTION OF CRUELTY TO CHILDREN, MY FAVOURITE CHARITY.

I EMPTY MY MIND WITH A THRILLER, AND REMEMBER THAT MOST THINGS ARE USUALLY SOLVED, IN THE END.

My Day by Sigmund Freud

7 A.M. I AWAKEN. I AM LIKE A WATCH THAT HAS NOT BEEN REPAIRED FOR A LONG TIME AND HAS GOT DUSTY IN ALL ITS PARTS. NO MORE CIGARS!

THOUGH AFTER A COLD SHOWER I FEEL IMMENSELY IMPROVED.

AND BY THE TIME I HAVE MY MORNING TRIM I AM MARKEDLY EUPHORIC.

8 A.M. THE ARRIVAL OF MY FIRST PATIENT— A VERY TALL HUNGARIAN. I BEGIN TO DEVELOP A MIGRAINE, BUT THIS IS PURELY EXTERNAL, THE INNER MAN IS INTACT.

I HELP MYSELF BY RENOUNCING ALL CONSCIOUS MENTAL EFFORT, BUT I HARDLY KNOW WHAT I AM DOING; BY WHICH TIME THE FIFTY-FIVE MINUTES ARE UP.

I TAKE A TWELVE MINUTE BREAK BETWEEN PATIENTS, AND THINK ABOUT SAVAGES AND NEUROTICS. I MUST WRITE TO JUNG, BUT NOT TOO MUCH.

MY NEXT PATIENT ARRIVES, ANOTHER HUNGARIAN. THE MAID TAKES HIS HAT AND COAT AND SAYS SOMETHING ABOUT THERE BEING THREE PEOPLE WAITING. I TELL HER NOT TO GET HYSTERICAL.

I P.M. I HAVE LUNCH WITH MY FAMILY. IT APPEARS THAT ONE OF THE CHILDREN IS NOT PRESENT. I DO NOT FEEL PARTICULARLY CONVERSATIONAL SO I POINT TO THE EMPTY SEAT IN QUESTION.

2 P.M. I TAKE MY DAILY CONSTITUTIONAL (AND BUY SOME CIGARS). I SHOULD BE TAKING PROOFS OF MY NEXT BOOK TO THE PUBLISHER, BUT I HAVE BEEN VERY IDLE.

THE MODERATE AMOUNT OF MISERY NECESSARY FOR INTENSIVE WORK HAS NOT SET IN, AND I HAVE BEEN TOO BUSY WITH MY ANTIQUITIES.

11 P.M. DINNER OVER, I TAKE A WALK WITH MY DAUGHTER AND SISTER-IN-LAW MINNA, BOTH VERY INTELLIGENT WOMEN.

FINALLY I RETIRE. ONE DREAMS SO AS NOT TO WAKE BECAUSE ONE WANTS TO SLEEP. TANT DE BRUIT.

My Day by Leonardo da Vinci

4 A.M. I WASH THOROUGHLY, ALTHOUGH I HAVE YET TO PERFECT MY "BATH PALACE".

I LEAVE MY PROTÉGÉ SALAINO TO HIS DREAMS. HE NEEDS HIS REST.

I AM DISAPPOINTED TO FIND THAT MY METHOD FOR WALKING ON WATER IS UNSUCCESSFUL. PERHAPS WITH A FEW MINOR ADJUSTMENTS...

WHILE I'M HERE, THOUGH, I JOT DOWN A FEW DETAILS ABOUT THE TRANSMISSION OF SOUND IN WATER,

AND CATCH A FEW FLIES.

SALAINO AND I CLIP THEIR WINGS, AND FIND THAT THIS CHANGES THEIR BUZZING!

SALAINO INFORMS ME THAT FRA PIETRO HAS LEFT A NOTE ASKING ME TO LUNCH. NOT ONLY WILL I NEVER FINISH MY MONA, BUT WHEN WILL I HAVE TIME FOR MY GEOMETRY?

ISABELLA D'ESTE INSISTS I PAINT HER PORTRAIT. HOW I HATE SOCIETY LUNCHEONS!

I HAVE TO KNOCK UP A TAPESTRY CARTOON FOR THE KING OF PORTUGAL BUT I'VE RUN OUT OF VARNISH SO I MAKE MY OWN. WHAT A WAY TO MAKE A LIVING!

MY LAST PATRON, LUDOVICO, MELTED DOWN SEVEN QUINTRELS OF BRONZE FOR CANNON JUST WHEN I WAS ALL SET TO CAST A LOVELY EQUESTRIAN STATUE.

THE HOUR IS LATE AND WITH ANY LUCK I WILL GET TO THE MORGUE UNNOTICED.

I WILL HAVE TO FINISH THE PLANS FOR ISABELLA OF ARAGON'S BATHROOM TOMORROW. THERE JUST AREN'T ENOUGH HOURS IN THE DAY!

My Day by Truman Capote

I AWAKEN, SORT OF. I FEEL LIKE A SOUTHERN BELLE WHO HAS LOST HER CRINOLINE.

I START MY NEXT BEST-SELLER. I AM PHYSICALLY INCAPABLE OF WRITING ANYTHING I WON'T BE PAID FOR.

WHEN GOD HANDS YOU A TALENT, HE ALSO HANDS YOU A WHIP...

I WRITE THE FIRST CHAPTER AND THE LAST. IT'S GOOD TO KNOW WHERE ONE IS GOING.

THE WHIP IS INTENDED SOLELY FOR SELF-FLAGELLATION

I REWRITE THE REWRITE OF THE LAST REWRITE AGAIN, UNTIL I REACH THE POETIC ALTITUDE FICTION IS CAPABLE OF REACHING. EVEREST.

WHY IS IT POSSIBLE FOR CAROLINE KENNEDY AND SANTA CLAUS TO GET INTO THE SAME PHONE BOOTH?

SAUVE BY THE BELL. A TELEPHONE CALL! SOMEONE IN THIS CITY IS STILL TALKING TO ME.

..BECAUSE SANTA CLAUS DOESN'T EXIST.

IT'S MY AGENT. HE HAS TO TALK TO ME. HE WANTS ME TO WRITE A PLAY. I REFUSE. I DON'T LIKE TEAM SPORTS.

IN COLD BLOOD

WHO WILL I BE TODAY? DANDY CAPOTE? WESTERN CAPOTE? I TRY ON A QUARTER OF MY HAT COLLECTION.

EVERYONE WANTS A TRUMAN IN HIS OR HER LIFE.

LUNCH WITH ONE OF MY BACK-UP GIRLS. I WON'T SAY WHICH ONE, BUT HER LAST NAME RHYMES WITH OIL WELL AND...

ANTIQ

I FEEL LIKE A FABERGE EGG. I WALK LUNCH OFF VISITING ANTIQUE SHOPS AND TAKING CREDIT CARDS IN AND OUT OF MY POCKET.

HE'S SO DUMB IT MAKES MY SKIN CRAWL

HOME AGAIN. I TRANSCRIBE AN INTERVIEW WITH MARLON BRANDO FROM MEMORY. I AM 92% ACCURATE TO HIS 100% HOT AIR.

HAVE YOU BEEN TO EUROPE?

ONLY WHEN I WENT TO VIETNAM.

OMIGOD BEAUTIFUL AND NEANDERTHAL

THE WORLD IS FULL OF MARRIED MEN. INSTEAD I TAKE A BEAUTIFUL BOY TO A BEAUTIFUL PARTY FOR BEAUTIFUL PEOPLE.

...AND SPARE ME FROM LUNCH ON THURSDAY AND EVER RUNNING INTO GORE VIDAL...

I SAY MY PRAYERS. MORE TEARS ARE SHED OVER ANSWERED PRAYERS THAN UNANSWERED ONES. GOODNIGHT.

My Day by Barbara Cartland

8:45 a.m. SHARP! I AM AWAKENED IN TIME FOR THE ROMANTIC BOOM.

VITAMINS, MINERALS AND A DASH OF RIBOFLAVIN FOR BREAKFAST TOPPED WITH HONEY KEEP ME SPLENDIDLY ALIVE!

I DRESS IN PINK PURELY TO PLEASE MYSELF. I DISCOVERED SIR NORMAN HARTNELL BEFORE THE QUEEN DID, AND VICE VERSA.

I WALK TWI TWI AND DUKE IN MY FOUR HUNDRED ENVIABLE ACRES OF PARK AND WOODLAND.

I DO A BIT OF RESEARCH, A BIT OF WRITING. (I DICTATE SEVEN THOUSAND WORDS)

I REMEMBER LORD BEAVERBROOK'S TIP "NEVER BE BORING" AND REDUCE MY PARAGRAPHS TO THREE LINES. IF THEY WERE ANY LONGER THE READER WOULD SKIP THEM.

MY PUBLISHER IS BEING A BORE — SOMETHING ABOUT OVEREXPOSURE AND GETTING CINDERELLA INTO BED BEFORE MARRIAGE.

I PHONE TWO NEW PUBLISHERS AND OFFER THEM TEN BOOKS A PIECE, THIS YEAR. EACH ACCEPTS, GRACEFULLY.

TO RELAX, I STROKE MY GILT ROCOCO TABLES. I COLLECT THEM. STAMPS ARE SO FIDDLY.

I ARRANGE A FUND-RAISING FOR GYPSIES. A VERITABLE SUCCESS. IT ALWAYS WORKS WHEN YOU SUGGEST TO PEOPLE THE QUALITIES YOU'D LIKE THEM TO POSSESS.

MY GOOD SON IAN DROPS BY. HE IS A VERY GOOD SON. HE RUNS CARTLAND PROMOTIONS.

THE PERFECT PARTY- DINNER WITH A MAN I FIND ATTRACTIVE AND WHO THINKS I'M WONDERFUL. HE BRINGS ME AN ORCHID, THE FEMININE MEDAL OF SUCCESS.

My Day by Beatrix Potter

8 A.M. I AM WOKEN BY MY HEDGEHOG, MRS. TIGGY WINKLE.

MY FATHER ASKS IF I SHOULD LIKE TO GO TO THE MUSEUM. I AM DELIGHTED.

FATHER NEVER INTRODUCES ME TO HIS FRIENDS, SO I'VE BROUGHT MY DRAWING PAD WITH ME.

WE TAKE TEA AND I THANK FATHER FOR THE OUTING. HE MIGHT TAKE ME OUT AGAIN IN THREE MONTHS' TIME.

UPON MY RETURN TO BOLTON GARDENS I FIND HUNCA MUNCA SWINGING FROM ONE OF THE CHANDELIERS.

I PUT HER BACK IN THE DOLLS' HOUSE WITH TOM THUMB. WE CAN ENGAGE IN MORE ACROBATICS LATER.

MRS. TIGGY WINKLE POSES FOR ME. SHE IS APT TO GET RATHER EVIL TEMPERED AND BITE AFTER TOO LONG, SO THIS WILL BE JUST A QUICK SKETCH.

I WRITE A LETTER TO MY PUBLISHER, NORMAN WARNE, TELLING HIM ABOUT MY NEXT STORY.

NORMAN IS SUCH A MARVELLOUS MAN. IT IS A SHAME THAT HE IS IN TRADE. FATHER WOULD NEVER APPROVE — BUT I AM THIRTY-SIX...

I ASK MRS. TIGGY WINKLE IF LIFE WAS MEANT TO BE LIKE THIS. SHE DOESN'T THINK SO.

I DRAW SOME ANTI FREE TRADE POSTERS TO TAKE MY MIND OFF THE PRESENT. WE CAN'T HAVE THE MARKET FLOODED WITH GERMAN PETER RABBIT DOLLS.

FINALLY, IT'S TIME TO RETIRE. I PUT MY FAMILY TO BED.

My Day by James Thurber

8 A.M. THE CLOCK SAYS: IT'S MORNING. I FEEL LIKE A SLIGHTLY ILL PROFESSOR OF BOTANY WHO IS ALSO LOST.

SO DOES MY ROOM. I'LL HAVE TO CHANGE HOTELS. I'M ALSO OUT OF CLEAN CLOTHES. I'LL HAVE TO BUY A NEW SUIT.

9 A.M. AT THE NEW YORKER, IN THE OFFICE WHERE E.B. WHITE AND I ALMOST FIT.

DOROTHY PARKER COMES BY, LOOKING FOR A PENCIL, BUT SHE CANNOT GET IN, NOR WILL SHE FIND A PENCIL. THEY WERE ALL GIVEN OUT LAST MONTH, THE WHOLE YEAR'S SUPPLY.

MY WIFE IS IN THE BAHAMAS AND I MISS MY DOGS. I DECIDE TO ASK MY BOSS ROSS FOR A NEW TYPEWRITER AND/OR A VACATION.

THE ANSWER IS TWO NOS. I DECIDE TO ORDER THE FANCIEST TYPEWRITER I KNOW AND CHARGE IT TO THE OFFICE.

1 P.M. LUNCH AT "TWENTY-ONE" WITH ANN HONEY-CUTT. WE START ARGUING AND I FEEL LIKE SLAPPING THIS SOUTHERN BELLE ACROSS THE TABLE.

I DO; AND SHE THROWS HER GLASS OF SCOTCH AT ME. WE ARE THROWN OUT AND END UP ON THE SIDEWALK.

BACK AT MY OFFICE I FIND MY NEW TYPEWRITER HAS ARRIVED. I THINK OF WHAT TO ORDER NEXT; ANDY SUGGESTS A NEW PHONE BOOTH.

I RIPPED THE OLD ONE OUT OF THE WALL LAST WEEK. I REALLY DO NEED A VACATION.

7 P.M. I FIND MYSELF BACK IN MY ROOM WITH THREE BEERS. I FEEL CHINLESS AND INEPT. I WOULD LIKE TO SEE HONEY (ANN).

LATER ON. I END UP AT THE BAR. I THINK ABOUT OHIO, AND MY MOTHER, AND HOW SHE USED TO PUT OUT FOOD FOR THE MICE. GOODNIGHT.

My Day by John (Joe) Orton

10:03 A.M. I AWAKEN. IT IS SUCH A PERFECT DAY (FOR LONDON), BEHIND THE VENETIANS, SEX SEEMS ALMOST IRRELEVANT.

10:04 A.M. I TAKE THAT SENTIMENT BACK. YOU MUST ENJOY SEX WHILE YOU'RE HERE. WHEN YOU'RE DEAD YOU'LL REGRET NOT HAVING FUN WITH YOUR GENITAL ORGANS.

KENNETH HALLIWELL HAS FINALLY AWAKENED. I DO THINK I'LL HAVE TO GET SOMETHING LARGER SOON. I WORK BETTER WHEN THERE'S SOMEONE WANDERING AROUND, BUT IT'S NOT FAIR TO THE OTHER PERSON...

THEY CAN'T READ AND IF THEY WANT TO TYPE ANYTHING THE PLACE SOUNDS LIKE A TYPING POOL. KENNETH'S LOOKING LIKE A ZOMBIE DOESN'T HELP EITHER.

KENNETH PRATTLES ON ABOUT WANTING A PLACE IN THE COUNTRY. HE'S GETTING TO BE AN EFFING MATER DOLOROSA. I POINT THIS OUT TO HIM.

HE REPLIES THAT I AM TURNING INTO A REAL BULLY AND THAT I WILL GET MY JUST DESSERTS AND THAT HOMOSEXUALS DISGUST HIM.
HE SHOULD HAVE MORE VALIUM AT MEALTIMES.

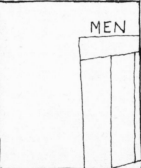

I POP INTO A LITTLE PISSOIR AND SOON FIND MYSELF IN A MOST UNAPPETISING POSITION FOR AN INTERNATIONALLY KNOWN PLAYWRIGHT TO BE IN.

STILL, ECSTASY IS AS LIABLE TO BORE AS BOREDOM. I RETURN HOME.

KENNETH IS FEELING BETTER. HE SERVES UP HIS SPECIALTY, RICE WITH SARDINES FOLLOWED BY RICE WITH GOLDEN SYRUP. HE SPOILS ME, REALLY.

I AM DEBATING WHICH IMAGINARY BOOK TITLE I LIKE BEST—"A STAG FOR NANNY," "THE PAINTED WHIP," "A COW CALLED ISIS"—WHEN KENNETH MENTIONS THAT HE HAS BUT ONE LITTLE WISH... TO BE LOVED.

I HAD NO IDEA OUR MARRIAGE TEETERED ON THE EDGE OF FASHION.

A HOLIDAY TO MOROCCO IS IN ORDER. PROVIDED ONE SPENDS THE TIME DRUGGED AND DRUNK, THE WORLD IS A FINE PLACE.

"My Day by Dorothy Parker

MORNING, CERTAINLY. I AWAKEN TO A WHISKY SOUR AND FOUR THINGS I'D BE BETTER WITHOUT: LOVE, CURIOSITY, FRECKLES AND DOUBT.

AND A FIFTH — DEADLINES. THE LAST TIME I WAS EARLY FOR ANYTHING WAS WHEN MY MOTHER BORE ME PREMATURELY. I TRY TO REVIEW THIS BOOK. IT MUST BE A GIFT BOOK BECAUSE NOBODY WOULD BUY IT ON ANY OTHER TERMS.

THE DOORBELL RINGS. WHAT FRESH HELL CAN THIS BE?

IT'S GEORGE OPPEN-HEIMER, WHO TRIES TO LOCK ME IN MY ROOM WITH A BOTTLE OF WHISKY AND MAKE HE CORRECT THE PAGE PROOFS FOR MY LATEST "LAMENTS OF THE LIVING".

I THOUGHT I HAD BURNT THEM.

I TELL HIM IT'S MY DAY OFF, AND THAT I'D RATHER GO TO A DOG SHOW SO THAT MY DOG CAN SEE OTHER DOGS.

WE ARRIVE AND THEY WON'T LET MY DOG IN LIKE THE OTHER GUESTS I DON'T SEE WHY, BUT I TAKE HER BACK TO THE CAR AND TELL HER IT'S ACTUALLY A FISH SHOW AND THAT SHE'S NOT MISSING OUT ON ANYTHING

HOME AGAIN. I AM JUST BECOMING SO BORED THAT I WOULD BE GLAD TO SEE F. SCOTT FITZ-GERALD AGAIN, WHEN MY LATEST BUSINESSMAN ARRIVES.

WE GO TO A PLAY. IN THE LAST ACT THE HEROINE IS STRANGLED BY ONE OF HER ADMIRERS. FOR ME, THE MURDER CAME TOO LATE.

AND SO IT DID ALAS, ALSO FOR MY BUSINESSMAN... I FIND HIM IN THE FOYER WITH SOMEONE ELSE. MY WORST SUSPICIONS ARE INVARIABLY CONFIRMED.

TOO BAD.

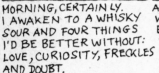

My Day by Noah

FIVE A.M.- MY SONS SHEM, HAM AND JAPHETH AND I ARE UP EARLY. WE HAVE MUCH TO DO BEFORE THE GREAT FLOOD, AND WE HAVE ONLY HAD SEVEN DAYS' NOTICE.

I MADE IT QUITE CLEAR TO THE BOYS, 300 × 50 × 30 CUBITS, BUT IT WOULD SEEM THAT GOPHER WOOD IS NOW SOLD IN METRIC. WE'VE GOT TO HURRY.

FURTHERMORE, THE PITCH IS NOT DRY YET, AND IT IS DUE TO START RAINING THIS AFTERNOON APPARENTLY.

"TWO OF EACH" SAID THE LORD. WE'LL HAVE TO EXTEND THE DOORWAY.

THE SNAILS HAVE YET TO TURN UP ... I DON'T KNOW WHERE THEY ARE.

AND MY WIFE REFUSES TO HAVE BATS ON BOARD.

WE CANNOT DISCRIMINATE, I TELL HER, AND SHE FINALLY AGREES TO HAVE THE BATS ON ANOTHER DECK. WE HAVEN'T MUCH TIME LEFT.

I ASK HER TO CHECK THAT WE HAVE EVERYTHING ON THE LIST OF EVERY FOOD THAT IS EATEN. WE ARE MISSING LEMON PEPPER ONLY.

I AM STILL WAITING FOR THE SNAILS AND HAM HAS ONLY MANAGED TO CAPTURE ONE EMU. IT IS GETTING LATE.

IT HAS STARTED DRIZZLING BUT MY SONS' WIVES STILL HAVE A FEW ODDS AND ENDS THEY CANNOT PART WITH.

WE ARE FINALLY ON BOARD.

OR ALMOST.

My Day by Robin Hood

'TIS A LOVELY BUT COLD MORNING IN SHERWOOD FOREST. I HASTEN TO THE RIVERSIDE AND TRIM MY PERFECTLY POINTED BEARD.

FRIAR TUCK AND I TAKE PART IN EARLY MORNING CALLISTHENICS. (HE WINS)

WE BREAKFAST. FRIAR TUCK HAS PURCHASED FRENCH PASTRIES AGAIN.

I AM RATHER PARTIAL TO THESE MYSELF, BUT MY KEEN VISION TELLS ME GUY OF GISBORNE IS A MILE AWAY.

I FOREGO THE BABA AU RHUM AND SUMMON MY MERRY MEN TO TAKE THEIR PLACES IN THE FOREST.

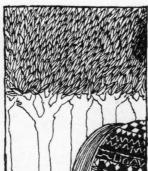

I CANNOT SEE THEM, SO THEY MUST BE IN PLACE.

GUY ACCUSES ME OF KILLING ONE OF HIS DEER. HE THREATENS TO IMPRISON ME (AND TAKE ALL MY LAND).

IT SEEMS A SHAME TO RUIN HIS SUNDAY BEST, BUT HE WILL MAKE ARROGANT THREATS.

MEANWHILE, BACK AT THE FARM, MAID MARION IS MAKING SCONES.

NEVER HAVE MY MERRY MEN BEEN MORE MERRY. I AM GLAD MARION ESCAPED THE NUNNERY.

IT IS LATE, AND I AM TIRED, BUT A FEW SERFS DROP BY AND TELL ME THEIR TROUBLES.

MAID MARION FIXES THE SERFS UP FOR THE NIGHT, AND WE RETIRE. TOMORROW IS, AFTER ALL, ANOTHER DAY.

My Day by Nancy Cunard

5:57 A.M. I AWAKEN AFTER A GHASTLY NIGHTMARE. I HAVE BEEN CAPTURED BY THE KLU KLUX KLAN FOR CULTIVATING "UN NOMBRE" OF NEGRO LOVERS. THEY TAKE AWAY MY AFRICAN BRACELETS AND FORCE ME TO LIVE IN ALABAMA.

BUT I COUNT THEM ALL AND THEY ARE ALL THERE AND I AM STILL IN LONDON — WHICH IS SURPRISING SINCE I CAN'T REMEMBER WHOM I HIT WITH THEM LAST NIGHT. WHOEVER IT WAS HIT ME BACK, BUT THERE'S ALWAYS A LITTLE VEIL.

GEORGE MOORE DROPS BY FOR BREAKFAST. HE WARNS ME THAT ULTIMATE GENIUS IS NOT IN EXPLOSIONS BUT IN RESTRAINTS. GEORGE IS A DEAR. I POUR US A GLASS OF WHITE WINE. HE TALKS ABOUT MY MOTHER.

HE MENTIONS SOMETHING ABOUT MUMMY BEING LONELY BETWEEN LUNCH AND DINNER ENGAGEMENTS. IT IS A PITY, BUT I AM A BIT TOO BUSY TO FIGURE OUT HOW MUCH OF A PITY IT IS.

MY NEGRO ANTHOLOGY MUST BE COMPLETED, EVEN IF SELLING THE BOOK TO ENGLISH PUBLISHERS WILL BE LIKE SELLING PERSIAN CARPETS TO MANURE MERCHANTS.

NEVER MIND, I'LL SOLVE THOSE COMPLICATIONS BY GETTING INTO OTHERS. IF ONLY I HADN'T INHERITED VITA SACKVILLE-WEST'S NANNY AS A CHILD. LONDON IS SO DREARY. REALLY.

I AM JUST ABOUT TO GO TO PARIS WHEN HENRY CROWDER ARRIVES FROM THE U.S. I WONDER IF HE INTENDS STAYING FOR LONG?

HE DOES. I MAKE SURE. "SOMEONE ELSE" PICKS UP HIS CLOTHING. A PITY, BUT IT'S NICE TO HAVE HENRY BACK AGAIN —

EVEN IF IT DOES MEAN SEEING "SOMEONE ELSE" IN A HOTEL. I SHOULD HATE IT, WERE LIFE TO BECOME REPETITIVE.

AFTER DINNER I FIND OUT THAT HENRY IS DEPRESSED. I SUGGEST HE GO TO ITALY, FIND A PIANO AND PRACTISE HIS MUSIC. THIS UPSETS HIM FOR SOME REASON, AND HE THREATENS TO GO BACK TO THE U.S.

THEN I REMEMBER HARLEM, THE HEAT, THE BEDBUGS, AMONG OTHER THINGS.

AND I GO BACK TO WORK ON MY ANTHOLOGY.

My Day by Evelyn Waugh

3 A.M. THREE HAIL MARYS HAVE DONE NOTHING FOR MY INSOMNIA. I TRY A SHAVE INSTEAD.

A SMOOTH FACE ON A SMOOTH PILLOW DOES, IN THEORY, INDUCE SLEEP, BUT IN WHOM?

8:05 A.M. ATLAST! MY WIFE LAURA HAS MANAGED TO PRODUCE ANOTHER ABOMINABLE BREAKFAST.

SO AWFUL IN FACT THAT I DECIDE IT IS TIME TO GET LIVE-IN HELP AGAIN-NONE OF THIS DAY HELP NONSENSE. WHAT IS HAPPENING TO THIS COUNTRY?!

I SEARCH THE MORNING PAPERS FOR A LIBELLOUS ARTICLE ON MYSELF. ONE NEVER KNOWS... AFTER ALL THE TAXMAN'S TAKEN ALL OF OUR MONEY, SO ONE MIGHT AS WELL SUE SOMEONE OR OTHER.

I WRITE MY MORNING POSTCARDS. THIS SOLVES ANY UNNECESSARY AND BORING PHONING TO PEOPLE ONE DOESN'T REALLY WANT TO TALK TO.

I RUN OUT OF GOSSIP AND DECIDE TO TAKE A WALK (FOR TWO HOURS). I SHOULD REALLY GO TO LONDON AND GATHER SOME NEW GOSSIP. I AM RUNNING OUT OF STORIES TO TELL.

3 P.M. I THINK ABOUT WRITING. IT SEEMS A WRITER HAS AT THE MOST THREE THEMES. I SEEM TO HAVE EXHAUSTED THE THREE.

LAURA SAYS SOMETHING ABOUT SCONES AND TEA, AND GUESTS. I SAY SOMETHING ABOUT WANTING NEITHER.

5 P.M. I AM FEELING IN HIGHER SPIRITS AFTER REVIEWING A WONDERFUL BOOK BY A RELATIVELY OBSCURE WRITER. I JOIN THE GUESTS, WHO APPEAR TO BE HOUSE GUESTS, AND OFFER THEM SOMETHING MORE INTERESTING THAN TEA.

8 P.M. I HAVE TAKEN OUT MY BEST BURGUNDY, AND AM DEBATING WHETHER OR NOT TO SERVE IT. IT APPEARS THESE HOUSEGUESTS DO NOT DRESS FOR DINNER.

AMERICANS I EXPECT, POOR BEASTS. I CONSUME YET ANOTHER FRIGHTFUL MEAL AND THINK ABOUT INSOMNIA.

My Day by Vita Sackville-West

ELEVEN A.M. VIOLET AND I HAVE BREAKFAST IN OUR LITTLE FLAT IN THE PALAIS ROYAL.

IT'S LOVELY TO BE BACK IN PARIS.

THOUGH I DO MISS MY GARDEN, SO I WATER LES PLANTES. VIOLET IS ON THE PHONE TO DENYS (DISCUSSING MARRIAGE)

VIOLET IS STILL ON THE PHONE... I CATCH UP ON HAROLD'S LETTERS FOR THIS WEEK.

VIOLET IS OFF THE PHONE, BUT DENYS WILL VISIT THIS AFTERNOON.

I ANSWER A FEW OF HAROLD'S LETTERS. I MISS MY HADJI. WE ARE SO HAPPY TOGETHER, AND YET...

VIOLET IS SO LATIN.

AND I'VE NEVER BEEN SO HAPPY. I CAN'T GO BACK TO ENGLAND FOR CHRISTMAS – PERHAPS NEXT MARCH.

DENYS HAS LEFT. WE HAVE A CUP OF TEA,

AND REMEMBER WE ARE IN PARIS! WE GET READY TO GO OUT.

I PUT ON A SUIT AND TURBAN AND BLACKEN MY FACE AND HANDS.

AND WE GO OUT TO MEET THE FRENCH. WHO WE ARE, THEY'LL NEVER KNOW.

My Day by Saint Benedict

DAWN - I HAVE A TERRIBLE NIGHTMARE. EUROPE IS IN A DESPERATE, DESPONDENT, DESPICABLE, DESTRUCTIVE AND DESULTORY STATE.

I RUN OUT OF D'S AND AWAKEN. I REALIZE I WAS NOT DREAMING.

I RENOUNCE THE HAPPINESS OF THIS WORLD. I SKIP BREAKFAST.

I FIND SHARP HILLS AND ABRUPT ROCK ONLY TWENTY FIVE MILES OUT OF ROME.

I FIND SHARPER HILLS AND RUDER ROCK FIFTY-TWO MILES OUT OF ROME.

MY CLOTHES ARE A MESS. I HIDE IN A DARK CAVE. BUT A MONK NAMED ROMANUS WHO ALSO TAILORS GIVES ME A HAIR SHIRT.

THESE GARMENTS FIT WELL, BUT I REMAIN IN MY CAVE, STRUGGLING WITH THE INFERNAL. I SKIP LUNCH.

A WOMAN WITH LIMITED DRESS SENSE TEMPTS ME, BUT I RESIST THE LURES OF VOLUPTUOUSNESS.

I ROLL ABOUT IN CLUMP OF BRIARS INSTEAD AND DISCOVER A BENT TOWARD GARDENING.

BETWEEN 4:30 AND 6:30 P.M. I TEACH OTHERS TO GARDEN. I ACQUIRE ONE DISCIPLE, THEN TWO, THEN THREE.

7:40 P.M. A DISCIPLE TRIES TO POISON ME (UNSUCCESSFULLY). I TOLD HIM THE COCKTAIL HOUR WAS PASSED.

9:05 P.M. I SUBDUE MYSELF AND STRUGGLE WITH THE INFERNAL; STRUGGLE WITH THE INFERNAL AND SUBDUE MYSELF; SUBDUE MYSELF AND... GOODNIGHT.

My Day by Eric Satie

DAWN. I ARRIVE HOME AFTER A NIGHT IN MONTMARTRE. TO FRESHEN UP I DON'T BATHE, PUMICE. PUMICE STONE IS BETTER THAN SOAP.

THREE MORCEAUX OF SOMETHING IN THE SHAPE OF A POIRE FOR BREAKFAST.

I AM DESTITUTE OF SOLS, DUCATS AND OTHER ARTICLES OF THAT KIND. I WRITE TO THE PRINCESSE DE POLIGNAC, MY DELIGHTFUL SPONSOR.

I FEEL BETTER. I WRITE A CHORALE FOR THE STUPID, PUTTING INTO IT ALL I KNOW ABOUT BOREDOM, AND DEDICATE IT TO ALL THOSE WHO DO NOT LIKE ME.

I DO MY COUNTERPOINT HOMEWORK FOR THE SCHOLA CANTORUM. MY TEACHER, MR. ROUSSEL, SAYS I'M DOING WELL... FOR A FORTY-YEAR-OLD.

I WEIGH THE WHOLE OF BEETHOVEN AND VERDI WITH MY INVENTION—THE PHONOMETER. AN ORDINARY F SHARP CAN WEIGH UP TO 93 KG.!!!!

A MEAL ON CREDIT AT NO. 15, COURTESY OF LA MÈRE TULARD. I SKIP THE SAUERKRAUT IT REMINDS ME OF WAGNER.

I TALK TO CHILDREN, THEY REMIND ME OF FUN.

THE MAILMAN HAS HAD THE GOOD GRACE TO DROP BY IN MY ABSENCE BEARING A ROYALTY CHEQUE FOR SEVENTY-SIX CENTIMES.

I EXCOMMUNICATE HIM (IN RED INK) FROM L'ÉGLISE MÉTROPOLITAINE D'ART DE JÉSUS CONDUCTEUR, MY CHURCH.

THEN I COMMUNICATE WITH THE POOR KNIGHTS OF THE HOLY CITY, MY KNIGHTS, IF ONLY I COULD AFFORD A ROUND TABLE.

TOO EARLY FOR MONTMARTRE AND/OR ABSYNTHE. I BEGIN WORK ON THE "LIFE OF SOCRATES" MY DRAME SYMPHONIQUE. GOODNIGHT DING DONG. CUCKOO. SALUT. BONSOIR.

My Day by Niccolò Machiavelli

7 A.M. I AWAKEN, ONLY TO REMEMBER THAT I AM OUT OF A JOB.

I CAN'T SEEM TO ADAPT TO MY CHANGING FORTUNA. I MISS POLITICS SO...

TO THINK I SPENT SO MANY YEARS IN LOYAL SERVICE TO THIS DISORGANIZED STATE (AND ON A LOW BUDGET) ONLY TO BE BANISHED TO MY COUNTRY ESTATE.

12 NOON. I HAVE AN IDEA. I STOP FEELING SORRY FOR MYSELF.

12:04 I BEGIN WRITING "THE PRINCE"— A HOW TO BOOK FOR RULERS. IT IS (WILL BE) THE GREATEST BOOK WRITTEN FOR YEARS.

MY WIFE AND I INDULGE IN PRE-LUNCH COCKTAILS, AND DRINK A TOAST TO LA FORTUNA. IF THIS BOOK GETS TO THE RIGHT MEDICIS I AM BOUND TO GET A JOB.

I HAVE A SIESTA AFTER LUNCH— I SHOULD REALLY BE WRITING. IT SEEMS THAT WHAT PEOPLE DO IS VERY DIFFERENT FROM WHAT THEY OUGHT TO DO...

ESPECIALLY PRINCES

BUT I DECIDE THAT THE MORE NECESSITA THERE IS, THE MORE VIRTU IN THE PRINCE THERE WILL BE. THIS CHEERS ME NO END...

EVEN IF THE ONLY PRINCE I CAN THINK OF WITH VIRTU IS CESARE BORGIA.

STILL, I KNOW SINGLE-MINDEDNESS IN ACTION IS THE KEY TO SUCCESS. I DECIDE TO GO TO BED.

I DREAM A STRANGE DREAM, SET FAR IN THE FUTURE. THERE ARE "PAPERBACK" EDITIONS OF THE PRINCE AND THEY ARE ALL MISUNDERSTOOD, YET PRINCES DO NOT SEEM TO HAVE CHANGED.

My Day by Michelangelo Buonarroti

6 A.M. - I AWAKEN. IN FRONT OF ME MY SKIN IS BEING STRETCHED WHILE IT FORMS UP BEHIND AND FORMS A KNOT, AND I AM BENDING LIKE A SYRIAN BOW.

I MUST HAVE BEEN DREAMING ABOUT THE SISTINE CHAPEL AGAIN. IF ONLY POPE JULIUS HAD GOT RAPHAEL TO DO IT.

IF IT WEREN'T FOR BRAMANTE'S "FRIENDLY" ADVICE TO POPE JULIUS I'D BE BUILDING HIS TOMB INSTEAD OF WORKING THE CEILING. WE HAD EVEN AGREED ON THE PRICE.

EVER SINCE I POINTED OUT THAT BRAMANTE CUTS COSTS HE'S BEEN INSUFFERABLE. BUT WHY ME? ANYONE CAN LOOK AT THE BELVEDERE CORRIDOR AND REALIZE IT'LL NEED A FEW FLYING BUTTRESSES TO KEEP IT STANDING—VERY SOON.

WHY DO PEOPLE CUT CORNERS? EVEN DONATELLO! HIS WORKS ARE ADMIRABLE WHEN SEEN FROM A DISTANCE BUT THEY LOSE THEIR REPUTATION WHEN SEEN FROM NEARBY.

I GO TO THE FISH MARKETS. IF I HAVE TO WORK WITH COLOUR INSTEAD OF MY BELOVED MARBLE, I'D MIGHT AS WELL GO TO THE SOURCE—FINS.

11:00 A.M. I FACE THE CEILING... I FACE MILDEW! THE FIGURES ON THE PICTURE OF THE FLOOD ARE BARELY DISTINGUISHABLE. THIS POSITIVELY PROVES I DON'T KNOW WHAT I'M DOING.

OH TO BE IN CARRARA! THERE I WOULD CARVE OUT OF A MOUNTAIN OVERLOOKING THE SEA A COLOSSUS WHICH WOULD BE VISIBLE FROM AFAR TO SEAFARERS.

3 P.M. I AM STILL FACING THE CEILING. I HAVE NO ASSISTANTS. WHO NEEDS ASSISTANTS TO MAKE YOUR LIFE MISERABLE WHEN POPE JULIUS IS IN TOWN?!

THE POPE HAS DISCOVERED RETOUCHING—HE'S DECIDED ON A SECCO WITH ULTRAMARINE AND IN A FEW PLACES GOLD TO GIVE THE CEILING A RICHER APPEARANCE.

11:00 P.M. ON MY WAY HOME I THINK OF GOING TO THE LEVANT. THE TURK HAS MADE MOST GENEROUS PROMISES THROUGH THE INTERMEDIARY OF CERTAIN FRANCISCAN FRIARS.

MIDNIGHT. I RETIRE TO THE COMPANY OF A GENTLEMAN WHO TREATS ME WITH GREAT HONOUR. WE READ FROM DANTE AND PETRARCH AND FINISH OFF WITH A LITTLE BIT OF BOCCACCIO.

My Day by Robinson Crusoe

5 A.M. I AM AWAKENED BY THE GOATS—

IT MUST BE FRIDAY, THERE IS NOBODY ABOUT; AT LEAST I HOPE NOT.

JUST THE THOUGHT OF NATIVES MAKES ME GRUESOMELY UNCOMFORTABLE. IN FACT, I HAVEN'T SLEPT WELL SINCE THE LAST BUNCH OF CANNIBALS WAS HERE TWO YEARS AGO.

I'VE FORGOTTEN MY PARASOL AND IT'S BEASTLY HOT. ACTUALLY IF ONE COULD CAPTURE A FEW OF THESE SAVAGES AND USE THEM AS SLAVES

I THINK I HEAR SOMETHING. OF COURSE, IT COULD JUST BE ME.

CANNIBALS! IS THIS PERCHANCE THE CHANCE THAT PROVIDENCE HATH PROVIDED ME WITH TO ACQUIRE A (OR MORE) SERVANT(S)?

OR SHALL I HIDE WHILE THERE IS STILL TIME? THERE'S ALWAYS MY HOUSE IN THE COUNTRY.

TOO LATE. THEY'RE HERE ALREADY, IN FACT ONE SEEMS TO BE RUNNING AWAY.

IT APPEARS I HAVE SAVED THIS MAN'S LIFE. HE IS ETERNALLY GRATEFUL.

WE HAVE TEA AND BISCUITS, AS I WAS NOT ENTHUSED AT MY MAN FRIDAY'S SUGGESTION THAT WE BRING HIS FRIENDS HOME FOR DINNER.

IT IS NICE TO HEAR ANOTHER MAN'S VOICE. I MUST TEACH FRIDAY SOME ENGLISH, HOW TO PLOUGH THE FIELD, MILK THE GOAT...

PLANT MY SEEDS, TRIM THE HEDGE, ETCETERA, AMONG OTHER THINGS, SO THAT I MAY DEDICATE MYSELF TO MORE ARTISTIC ENDEAVOURS.

My Day — by Isak Dinesen [Karen Blixen]

6 A.M. - I DISCARD BREAKFAST. BEING OVERWEIGHT CRAMPS MY STYLE, THE BEING ME.

I DON'T FEEL WELL - IS IT MALARIA, RHEUMATISM, LUMBAGO, OR SOMETHING FOR MY VENEREOLOGIST DR. RASCH? THANK THE LORD FOR FARAH, MY SHORT SOMALI.

I PROMISED THE DEVIL MY SOUL AND HE PROMISED ME THAT EVERYTHING HEREAFTER WOULD BE TURNED INTO TALES...

OR LETTERS. I WRITE FIVE OF THEM TO AUNT BESS, BACK HOME IN DENMARK. MY FAMILY WANTS ME TO COME HOME. IF I WANT A CHANGE OF AIR I'LL GO ON SAFARI.

I DISCARD LUNCH, PAINT A KIKUYU INSTEAD. A BAD CHOICE. KIKUYUS FEAR IMMOBILITY MORE THAN DEATH.

DENYS FINCH HATTON DROPS BY ON HIS WAY TO TANGANYIKA, FOR SEVEN HOURS. THE VALUE OF PLEASURE LIES SURELY IN ITS RARITY... AND BREVITY.

WE GO FOR A DRIVE AND FIND A LION. WE SIMPLY MUST HAVE IT. WE DO. WE HAVE THREE.

WE RETURN TO FIND LORD DELAMERE HITTING GOLF BALLS ONTO OUR ROOF. IT'S A SHAME DENMARK DOESN'T HAVE A COLONY. THE ENGLISH ARE PARTICULARLY FOREIGN TO ME.

WE DRESS FOR DINNER. I WEAR THE NEW SHOES I HAD MADE FROM AFRICAN SNAKESKINS AT HELLSTERN'S IN PARIS.

ISMAIL, MY SOMALI COOK, IS FINALLY GETTING OVER THE TRAINING HE RECEIVED FROM HIS PREVIOUS MISTRESS - AN ENGLISHWOMAN.

AFTER DINNER, DENYS BUTTS ARMCHAIRS OVER LIKE A BULL, THEN SITS IN THEM. HE LIKES TO DO THAT.

WE READ SHELLEY ALOUD. I BREAK THE TEN COMMANDMENTS AND FIND MUCH PLEASURE IN DOING SO.

My Day by Anaïs Nin

9 A.M. I ALLOW MYSELF TO DREAM LATE.

I AM FINALLY WAKENED TO ANOTHER DAY OF CREATION.

MY FRIEND GONZALO AND I HAVE BREAKFAST. HE MENTIONS THAT HE IS AN ARTIST AND I TRANSLATE VOL. I OF MY JOURNALS INTO ENGLISH.

HE INSISTS WE GO FOR A WALK AND TAKES ME TO THE GIPSY QUARTER WHERE I MEET DJANGO REINHARDT. THERE IS SUCH LIGHT, SUCH ATMOSPHERE. HERE I COULD WRITE...

GONZALO INSISTS I ACCOMPANY HIM TO A COMMUNIST RALLY. IT IS ALL VERY INTERESTING BUT I CAN NEVER BE TOTALLY COMMITTED-THE ME, THE ANAÏS, ALWAYS TAKES OVER IN THE END.

GONZALO DEVOURS HIS SALADE NIÇOISE WHILE I PONDER OVER MY DESIRE FOR ADVENTURE, EXPANSION, FEVER, FANTASY, GRANDEUR, BUT I AM HAVING DINNER WITH HENRY MILLER.

I INDULGE IN AN AFTERNOON DREAM, AND WAKE TO FIND HENRY AT THE DOOR. HE HAS BEEN POSING FOR BRASSAI ALL AFTERNOON.

HE LOOKS THROUGH HIS LETTERS TO ME IN SEARCH OF AN INTRODUCTION TO HIS NEXT CHAPTER. HE IS STILL WRITING LIKE A MANIAC ABOUT SEX, I ASSUME.

I GO THROUGH HIS LATEST PIECE. IT IS SUPERB, BUT NEEDS SOME REORGANIZING. I PROMISE TO LEND HIM MY TYPEWRITER,

AND DO A FEW OTHER ODDS AND ENDS (6) FOR HIM.

GOODBYE

LARRY AND NANCY DURRELL ARRIVE FOR DINNER. THEY ARE ANXIOUS TO GET BACK TO GREECE,

AND I TOO, AM ANXIOUS TO GET BACK TO MY DIARY AND BACK TO MY DREAMS. BONSOIR MES PETITS.

My Day by Isadora Duncan

POST·DAWN· I AWAKEN. MY SOUL IS LIKE A BATTLEFIELD WHERE APOLLO, DIONYSUS, CHRIST, NIETZCHE, AND RICHARD WAGNER DISPUTE THE GROUND.

ON TOP OF WHICH, I HAVE A BURNING DESIRE TO SEE ATHENS AGAIN. BUT I CANNOT BE OTHER THAN A MODERN. I COULD NOT HAVE THE FEELING OF THE ANCIENT GREEKS.

I AM, AFTER ALL, BUT A SCOTCH-IRISH-AMERICAN.

IN MY WHITE TUNIC I SIP WHITE MILK AND POUR OVER KANT'S CRITIQUE OF PURE REASON, FINDING INSPIRATION FOR THOSE MOVEMENTS OF PURE BEAUTY WHICH I SEEK. THEN MY STUDENTS ARRIVE. I PUT UP THE DRAPES.

MY GIRLS! NOW RESEMBLING A POMPEIIAN FRIEZE, NOW THE YOUTHFUL GRACES OF DONATELLO, OR, AGAIN, THE AIRY FLIGHTS OF TITANIA'S FOLLOWING; I TEACH THEM TO WEAVE AND ENTWINE, TO PART AND UNITE, IN ENDLESS ROUNDS AND PROCESSIONS. ONE DAY I WILL HAVE A VAST SCHOOL AND MY GIRLS WILL DANCE TO THE NINTH SYMPHONY OF BEETHOVEN IN THE DANCE THAT WILL BE THE DIVINE EXPRESSION OF THE HUMAN SPIRIT THROUGH THE MEDIUM OF THE BODY'S MOVEMENT.

BEAUTY IS TRUTH, TRUTH BEAUTY—THAT IS ALL YE KNOW ON EARTH AND ALL YE NEED TO KNOW—UNTIL YOU ARE EVICTED. I NEED A MILLIONAIRE. IT WOULD SIMPLIFY THINGS.

UNLIKE GORDON CRAIG, WHO COMPLICATES EVERYTHING. HE WONDERS WHY I WANT TO GO ON STAGE AND WAVE MY ARMS ABOUT WHEN I COULD STAY AT HOME AND SHARPEN HIS PENCILS.

BUT ART CALLS. TONIGHT I AM THE FIFTY DANAÏDES. I FEEL INADEQUATE AS THE FIFTY DANAÏDES, AND EXPLAIN TO THE PUBLIC THAT I SHOULD REALLY NOT BE MYSELF BUT FIFTY MAIDENS.

MY CHORUS OF YOUNG GREEKS IS OFF KEY AND ONE CAN NO LONGER EXCUSE IT ON THE GROUNDS THAT IT IS BYZANTINE.

I RETIRE. MY SOUL IS LIKE A BATTLEFIELD WHERE APOLLO, DIONYSUS, CHRIST, NIETZCHE, AND RICHARD WAGNER DISPUTE THE GROUND... STILL.

My Day by Patrick White

I RISE WITH THE BIRDS... AND THE DOGS

MIND YOU, I'M LESS VAIN SINCE LOSING MY TEETH.

I LOOK OLD — THE PRICE A NOVELIST PAYS FOR LIVING SO MANY LIVES IN ONE BODY.

EXOTICA! NOT MUESLI AGAIN!! I WANTED BOUREKAKIA.

A SOLID BREAKFAST FOR MY SOLID MANDALA.

SO THAT, IN THE END, THERE IS NO END.

I WAS DRAWN TO GREECE FROM A DISTANCE AND ONE GREEK IN PARTICULAR. THE GREEK FATALITY IS ALSO MY OWN. I DO THE DISHES.

THERE WOULD BE NO LIFE OR WORK IF I SAT AROUND DISCUSSING THESE! SHOOO!

MISOGYNIST!

AN INTRUDER — WORSE! A JOURNALIST! IT WANTS TO DISCUSS MY LIFE AND WORK. THAT'S WHAT I GET FOR WINNING THE NOBEL PRIZE.

32½ INVITATIONS TO LUNCH, AND "HOLIDAY ON ICE" WANT TO DO VOSS!

EXTRAORDINARY MAIL. IF I HAVE NOT LOST MY MIND I CAN SOMETIMES HEAR IT PREPARING TO DEFECT.

NUNS FART. WHY, EVEN STRAVINSKY...

I FINISH THE VACCUUMING AND CONCENTRATE ON MY FAVOURITE SUBJECT — DECAY.

SEE YOU UNDER THE PERGOLA — SOON!

BLAH BLAH BLAH

THE PURITAN IN ME WRESTLES WITH THE SENSUALIST. THEN THE PHONE RINGS. I LOVE THE PHONE ALMOST AS MUCH AS I LOVE MY PRE-LUNCH VODKA.

HE'S PAINTED YOU AS HALF-PIG, HALF-FLEA, AND NEVER MIND WHAT HE'S DONE TO ME!

NASTY SIR NED KELLY NOLAN OF HEREFORD, U.K., HAS BEEN BEHAVING IN THE MOST EXTRAORDINARY WAY. MUST BE A SIDE EFFECT OF HIS IRISH CHARM.

HOW COULD SID BEHAVE SO ABOMINABLY? AND HOW COULD I NOT INCLUDE THIS IN MY AUTOBIOGRAPHY?

BUT I RECOVER, AS FROM ALL THE CUPS OF VINEGAR I HAVE BEEN FORCED TO DRINK IN LATER LIFE... EARLIER LIFE... MIDDLE LIFE.

I LOVED YOUR CHARIOTS OF FIRE!

I RATION MYSELF SOCIALLY — ONE GALLERY OPENING FULL OF OUT-OF-THE-CUPBOARD QUEENS AND PEOPLE TO WHOM ONE SAYS "HELLO" AND "GOODBYE"!

GOD GAVE US MEAT. WE HAVE TO GO TO THE DEVIL FOR SAUCE!

SPAGHETTI ON A STEAMY SYDNEY SUMMER'S EVE. I REMEMBER MY MOTHER RUTH AND HOW AFTER TEN YEARS OF CULTIVATING HER FIGURE, SHE FINALLY TOOK TO TUCKING IN.

My Day by Salvador Dali

6 A.M. I AWAKEN. CREATIVE DREAMS ALL NIGHT. IN ONE OF THEM, I INVENTED A COMPLETE DRESS COLLECTION, ITSELF SUFFICIENT TO ASSURE MY FORTUNE THROUGH SEVEN SEASONS.

I LOVE US BOTH SO MUCH!

COFFEE, CREAM AND A SARDINE WITH GALA. GALA GRADIVA, GALATEA PLACIDA, GALA MY TREASURE! IT MUST BE DIFFICULT FOR OTHER PEOPLE, NOT BEING GALA OR SALVADOR DALI.

I POUR OVER MY HEAD THE OIL THAT IS LEFT FROM MY CAN OF SARDINES. OF ALL THE SYBARITIC PLEASURES OF MY LIFE LYING IN THE SUN COVERED BY FLIES IS THE MOST STIMULATING.

AN EXCEPTIONAL DEFECATION—TWO SMALL TURDS IN THE SHAPE OF RHINOCEROS HORNS!

I START PAINTING AS A NIGHTINGHALE SINGS. I SUCCEED IN MAKING A BRUSHSTROKE THAT IS EVANGELICALLY MIRACULOUS.

I HAVE TO PAINT WELL. MY NUCLEAR MYSTICISM CAN ONLY TRIUMPH ON THE APPOINTED DAY ONLY IF IT IS INCARNATED IN THE MOST SUPREME BEAUTY.

I AM SURREALISH!

THE SURREALISTS EXPELLED ME BECAUSE I WAS TOO SURREALIST. IN DREAMS ONE COULD USE SADISM, UMBRELLAS AND SEWING MACHINES AT WILL, BUT THEY DISLIKED ANUSES.

THE SIMPLEST WAY NOT TO HAVE TO MAKE CONCESSIONS TO GOLD IS TO HAVE IT ONESELF

A PARADISIACAL PAUSE. I THINK ABOUT GOLD. PERHAPS IT IS THE PHOENICIAN SIDE OF MY AMPURDAN BLOOD THAT MAKES ME SO FOND OF SO MUCH OF IT.

VISITORS, A WASTE OF PRECIOUS TIME!

GOLDEN THOUGHTS RUDELY INTERRUPTED BY THE VISIT OF AN UNKNOWN GENTLEMAN. I DO NOT WANT TO SEE HIM. BUT, IF HE SO PASSIONATELY, DESPERATELY WANTS TO SEE ME, I SUPPOSE...

A BALLET A PHILOSOPHY, A NEW WAY TO PEE!

MR. X. TURNS OUT TO BE A WHALEMAN. I REQUEST HIM TO SEND ME SEVERAL VERTEBRAE OF THE MAMMAL. IN LESS THAN AN HOUR I HAVE LISTED 62 DIFFERENT APPLICATIONS FOR THESE WHALE VERTEBRAE. I AM FULL OF IDEAS.

WE ARE ALL THIRSTY FOR CONCRETE IMAGES.

I SEE A WOMAN, DRESSED AS A TORERO BALANCING AN OMELETTE AUX FINES HERBES UPON HER HEAD. DINNER IS SERVED.

NIGHT STARS USED TO MAKE ME MELANCHOLY BECAUSE MY EMOTIONS WERE INDEFINABLE. NOW MY EMOTION IS SO DEFINABLE THAT I COULD MAKE A CAST OF IT. IN FACT I DECIDE TO RENDER ONE IN PLASTER TOMORROW.

My Day by Andy Warhol

I AWAKEN. I CAN'T REMEMBER THE DAY BEFORE. MAYBE I'M STILL AT THE PARTY I WASN'T AT THE NIGHT BEFORE. OR MAYBE I'VE FINALLY GOT MY OWN T.V. SHOW CALLED "NOTHING SPECIAL", AND WE'RE TAPING.

I LOOK IN THE MIRROR AND I SEE NOTHING. PEOPLE SAY I AM A MIRROR, AND IF A MIRROR LOOKS INTO A MIRROR, WHAT IS THERE TO SEE?

SUDDENLY I SEE A LOT! A NEW PIMPLE !!! I APPLY THE FLESH-COLOURED ACNE PIMPLE MEDICATION THAT DOESN'T RESEMBLE ANY FLESH I'VE EVERSEEN, THOUGH IT DOES RESEMBLE MINE.

THE PIMPLE'S COVERED, BUT AM I COVERED? I LOOK IN THE MIRROR FOR SOME MORE CLUES. NOTHING IS MISSING, IT'S ALL THERE— THE DIFFRACTED GAZE, THE BORED LANGUOR, THE CHIC FREAKINESS.

I WISH I COULD INVENT SOMETHING LIKE BLUEJEANS. SOMETHING TO BE REMEMBERED FOR. SOMETHING "MASS".

I PAINT INSTEAD. QUANTITY IS THE BEST GAUGE ON ANYTHING. YOU'RE ALWAYS DOING THE SAME THING, EVEN IF IT LOOKS LIKE YOU'RE DOING SOMETHING ELSE. PICASSO DID FOUR THOUSAND MASTERPIECES IN HIS LIFETIME.

BUSINESS ART IS THE STEP THAT COMES AFTER ART. MAKING MONEY IS ART AND WORKING IS ART AND GOOD BUSINESS IS THE BEST ART.

A BREAK FROM MONOTONY. LUNCH WITH THIRTEEN OF THE MOST BEAUTIFUL WOMEN IN THE WORLD... AND EIGHT PEOPLE FROM THE OFFICE TO DISTRACT THEM FROM ME.

I ORDER EVERYTHING I DON'T WANT. I ASK FOR A DOGGIE BAG THEN I LEAVE IT OUT IN THE STREET FOR A FELLOW NEW YORKER. I BELIEVE IN RECYCLING.

I ALSO BELIEVE IN LOW LIGHTS AND TRICK MIRRORS. IF YOU LEARN ABOUT SEX WHEN YOU'RE FORTY YOU'D BETTER BELIEVE IN LOW LIGHTS AND TRICK MIRRORS.

PEOPLE ARE ALWAYS LOOKING FOR SOMEONE TO BE THEIR "VIA VENETO", THEIR SOUFFLE THAT CANNOT FALL. I MARRIED MY TAPE RECORDER IN 1961 AND I'M HAVING AN AFFAIR WITH FOUR TELEVISION SETS.

SOMEHOW, THE WAY LIFE WORKS, PEOPLE USUALLY WIND UP EITHER IN CROWDED SUBWAYS AND ELEVATORS OR IN BIG ROOMS ALL BY THEMSELVES. GOODNIGHT.

My Day by Gertrude Stein

6 A.M. ALICE IS UP MAKING BAGELS. IT IS THE COOK'S DAY OFF.

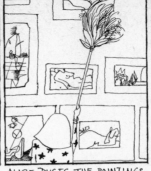
WE HAVE BREAKFAST.

ALICE DUSTS THE PAINTINGS.

I SETTLE DOWN TO SOME SERIOUS WRITING. THIS SENTENCE IS NOT QUITE CLEAR. I SHALL REPEAT IT FIVE TIMES AND GET MY MEANING ACROSS.

MY BROTHER LEO DROPS IN FOR ELEVENSES. ALICE HAS JUST COOKED UP SOME POPPYSEED BLINTZES FROM SCRATCH. HE IS TROUBLED.

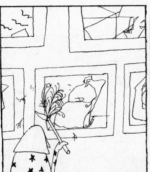
ALICE CONTINUES TO DUST THE PAINTINGS.

I DO MY GARDENING.

AN UNWANTED GUEST ARRIVES.

PABLO AND HIS LATEST, FERNANDE, ARRIVE FOR DINNER. FERNANDE REFUSES TO REMOVE HER NEW HAT DURING THE MEAL.

THE GUESTS LEAVE. MY BROTHER LEO DROPS BY FOR A POST-PRANDIAL CHAT. I TELL HIM NOT TO WORRY. IT IS NOT EASY HAVING A SISTER WHO IS A GENIUS.

ALICE FINISHES DUSTING THE PAINTINGS.

I SETTLE DOWN TO TONIGHTS SENTENCE.

My Day by Eva Perón

6 A.M.– I AWAKEN. I TOUCH UP MY WORKING CLASS ROOTS, AMONG OTHER THINGS.

7 A.M., IN THE "FUR ROOM" WITH MY BROTHER, JUAN DUARTE. HE USED TO BE IN THE SOAP BUSINESS. NOW HE'S PERON'S PRIVATE SECRETARY. WE DECIDE WHAT I SHOULD WEAR AND WHOM PERON SHOULD SEE.

9 A.M. BREAKFAST IN THE HAT ROOM WITH MY PRESIDENT. I WISH HE WOULDN'T PUT POMADE ON HIS CHIN. WE DISCUSS WHAT NEWSPAPER TO GIVE PRINTER'S INK TO NEXT WEEK.

IT'S MY SECRETARY LILIANE GUARDO'S DAY OFF. I SEND A LIMOUSINE TO FETCH HER. MOTHER AND I COULDN'T SHOP AT RICCIARDI'S WITHOUT HER. SHE HAS TASTE.

I'M IN A RING MOOD. I CAN'T DECIDE WHICH ONE I LIKE THE BEST. I TAKE THEM ALL. PITY ONE ONLY HAS TEN TINY FINGERS.

LUNCH WITH MEMBERS OF THE PERONIST WOMEN'S PARTY. I NEED GOOD PERONISTS - FANATICS. NOT THOSE FEMINISTS WHO HAVE TROUBLE BEING WOMEN. ALL OF MY BATHROBES ARE FROM PARIS.

3 P.M. I MANAGE TO PAVE THE PLAZA DE MAYO WITH PEOPLE, AGAIN. PERON'S SPEECH RUNS OUT. I AD LIB. I HAVE PLAYED QUEEN ELIZABETH I, SARAH BERNHARDT, THE LAST TSARINA.

WHEN THE RICH LOOK AFTER THE POOR THEY HAVE POOR IDEAS. NOW I LOOK AFTER THE POOR AT THE EVA PERON FOUNDATION. I ANSWER 12,000 LETTERS ASKING FOR HELP AND GIVE OUT FIFTY PESO BILLS UNTIL I RUN OUT FOR SOME REASON.

NOT TO WORRY. A "SPONTANEOUS DONATION" FROM MU MU THE SWEETMAKERS ARRIVES. THEY HADN'T GIVEN ANYTHING TO OUR FOUNDATION UNTIL WE DISCOVERED RATS HAIRS IN THEIR CARAMEL VATS.

8 P.M. A SPOT OF TROUBLE. A SHIPMENT OF VACCINE VIALS FROM THE FOUNDATION HAS GONE OUT WITHOUT MY INITIALS ON EVERY VIAL. REALLY!

NO PREMIÈRES TONIGHT, PITY. BUT I ALWAYS ENJOY THE PEÑA EVA PERON, A GROUP WHICH WRITES POEMS AND RECITES POEMS ABOUT ME CONSTANTLY.

MIDNIGHT. I CONFESS TO MY PRIEST. MOTHER'S GONE TO MAR DEL PLATA TO THE CASINO. I'LL HIRE SOMEONE TO CARRY HER CHIPS, TOMORROW. SHE DROPS THEM ALL.

My Day by Alfred Hitchcock

9 A.M. I AWAKEN, ONLY TO FIND THAT I HAD ALREADY WOKEN EARLIER AND HAD BREAKFAST.

I WOULDN'T MIND BREAKFAST AGAIN. I HAVE A BIT OF DOVER SOLE AND ENGLISH BACON LEFT IN MY WALK-IN FREEZER. ALMA HANDS ME A CUP OF BLACK TEA.

I THROW THE CUP OVER MY SHOULDER. ALMA IS SURPRISED. WOULDN'T YOU DO THE SAME ON 500 CALORIES A DAY?

I MOP UP AFTER MYSELF. ALMA HAS A SORE THROAT. SHE HASN'T BEEN THE SAME SINCE SHE KISSED THE POPE'S RING SEVERAL YEARS AGO.

I DRIVE MY DAUGHTER TO MASS. ANYBODY IS MAD TO DRIVE IN AMERICA UNLESS IT IS TO AND FROM MASS.

ONE CAN BE ALONE IN A CROWD OF THE FRIENDLIEST PEOPLE. MY DAUGHTER LEAVES FOR THE CONFESSIONAL. I FALL ASLEEP.

I DON'T KNOW IF I AM AWAKE OR ASLEEP, BUT A VISION OF A STATUE CRACKING TO REVEAL INGRID BERGMAN COVERED IN ANTS OVERTAKES ME.
PITY SALVADOR DALI IS PRESENTLY WORKING ON A FEATURE FOR WALT DISNEY.

I READ A NICE BLUE BOOK. BLUE IS SUCH A PRETTY COLOUR. I CAN'T UNDERSTAND WHY MORE OF THE THINGS WE EAT AREN'T BLUE.

EDWARD IX AND PHILLIP OF MAGNESIA ANNOUNCE THE ARRIVAL OF A GUEST.

MAYBE IT WASN'T A GUEST AT ALL. SINCE MY WIFE TRADED OUR MONEY TREE FOR A GIFT COUPON TREE STRANGERS HAVE TRIED TO BRAVE THE FENCE OFTENER THAN EVER.

8 P.M. I RETIRE AND READ ANOTHER BOOK, A GREEN ONE THIS TIME. GREEN IS SUCH A PRETTY COLOUR. SALADS.

My Day by Radclyffe Hall

7 A.M. IT IS REALLY TOO LATE AND TOO EARLY TO GO TO BED. IF CHRONIC INSOMNIA WERE THE MARK OF BRILLIANCE I WOULD BE A GENIUS.

I SUGGEST TO UNA TROUBRIDGE THAT I MIGHT LIKE TO GO FOR A WALK. SHE SUGGESTS THAT IF I DO THAT, AND BEFORE BREAKFAST, SHE WILL WALK AROUND FLORENCE IN HER PYJAMAS.

INSTEAD UNA READS TO ME ALOUD WHAT I HAVE JUST WRITTEN. IT IS NOT SO MUCH THAT I LIKE BEING READ TO ALOUD, BUT THAT UNA CAN DECIPHER MY HANDWRITING.

IT'S AS DEAD AS QUEEN ANNE!!!

I HAVE BARELY BUTTERED MY FIRST CROISSANT WHEN I REALIZE THE SECOND DRAFT IS WORSE THAN THE FIRST.

FURTHER DRAMA ENSUES WHEN UNA DISCOVERS I DESTROYED THE FIRST DRAFT (BY FIRE). I PUT THE FISH IN THE BATH FOR THEIR DAILY EXERCISE.

GRRRRR

I TAKE TULIP FOR A WALK. MARY ROSE IS NO LONGER WITH US. WE WERE FORCED TO MAKE A GIFT OF HER TO AN ITALIAN COUNTESS WHEN SHE ATTACKED A NUN.

GRRRRARK

UNA IS IN A BETTER MOOD. SHE HAS FOUND A SPOT FOR MY OLD HORSE JOSEPH'S HOOVES, JUST ABOVE THE FIREPLACE.

IT IS AT LUNCH THAT I AM SUDDENLY INSPIRED! I AM GOING TO WRITE ABOUT A WAITER WHO BECOMES SO UTTERLY SICK OF HANDLING FOOD THAT HE PRACTICALLY LETS HIMSELF DIE OF STARVATION...

AFTER LUNCH, UNA WRITES FOR THE SOCIETY FOR PSYCHICAL RESEARCH. SHE ASKS IF, AFTER MY DEATH, WERE SHE STILL ALIVE, SHOULD SHE ATTEMPT TO CONTACT ME,

WOULD I RESPOND? I, OF COURSE, WOULD DO MY UTMOST TO RESPOND.

WE GO TO MASS AND CEASE WORRYING ABOUT THE HEREAFTER.

UNA SUGGESTS I GET A BIT OF REST. SHE IS RIGHT, AS USUAL. I DO EXACTLY THE OPPOSITE.

My Day by Ludwig Van Beethoven

5 A.M. I AWAKEN WITH A BUZZING IN MY EARS...

AND COLIC. MY QUACK HAS SUGGESTED A COLD BATH AS A SOLUTION. IT ISN'T.

MY VALET BRINGS IN MY SUIT— BUT THIS IS NOT THE SAME ONE I HAVE BEEN WEARING FOR THREE WEEKS, IN FACT IT ISN'T MINE AT ALL!

STILL; IT'S NOT TOO BAD. WHOEVER IS LEAVING ME SUITS IN THE NIGHT HAS EXCELLENT TASTE. I WON'T WONDER WHO IT IS.

I GET SOME FRESH AIR, WEARING MY HAT, A GIFT FROM PRINCE LICHNOWSKY. I THINK I AM GOING DEAF.

IT'S AS THOUGH, OUT HERE, EVERY TREE SAYS TO ME, "HOLY, HOLY!" SO WHAT IF I'M GOING DEAF!

THE BUZZING CONTINUES, BUT SO MUST MY WORK. MOZART'S BROTHER-IN-LAW IS SINGING AT PRINCE LOBKOWITZ' TONIGHT.

I MUST COOK UP SOMETHING SPECIAL (TRICKY). WHAT FUN! HERE'S SOME TROUBLE FOR THE SECOND HORN TOO.

EN ROUTE TO THE PRINCE'S I HEAR A BLIND BOY FUMBLING AT THE PIANO. I INTRODUCE MYSELF AND MAKE UP THE MOONLIGHT SONATA.

I AM READY TO CONDUCT, THEN I REALISE WE ARE SHORT ONE BASSOON. WHO DOES THIS LITTLE ROYAL FITZLIPUTZLI THINK I AM???

DISGUSTED, I LEAVE THE PRINCE'S AND HAVE DINNER WITH A DEAR, FASCINATING GIRL INSTEAD.

FINALLY I RETIRE. THERE IS STILL A BUZZING IN MY EARS. I AM NOT AT ALL SATISFIED WITH MY WORK THOUGH, AND I WILL MAKE A FRESH START... TOMORROW.

My Day by Franz Kafka

7 A.M. I AWAKEN. THERE IS STILL SUCH A THICK FOG. HOW MELANCHOLY.

NOT ONLY THAT, BUT I SEEM TO HAVE DEVELOPED INTO A HORRIBLE CREATURE.

I TRY TO GET OUT OF BED. I HAVE ALREADY MISSED ONE TRAIN AND I WILL BE LATE FOR WORK.

I WILL LOSE MY JOB AND MY MOTHER WILL HAVE TO MAKE UNDERWEAR FOR STRANGERS.

I AM HAVING TROUBLE WITH THE DOOR (I NO LONGER HAVE TEETH) UNTIL THE CHARWOMAN ARRIVES. SHE TELLS ME IT'S SUNDAY, NOT TO BOTHER GETTING UP.

AND SUMMONS MY PARENTS. THEY ARE UPSET AT THIS IRREGULAR MISFORTUNE WHICH HAS BEFALLEN THEM.

THEY DISCUSS IT OVER BREAKFAST. THE COOK RESIGNS.

MY SISTER BRINGS ME SOME BREAD AND MILK, BUT I NO LONGER LIKE BREAD OR MILK.

IT'S STILL RAINING. I THINK ABOUT MY FAMILY. THEY'LL NEVER BE ABLE TO AFFORD TO SEND MY SISTER TO THE CONSERVATORIUM.

IF ONLY I COULD WRITE, BUT I CAN'T EVEN HOLD A PEN. PERHAPS I COULD EARN A LIVING AS A LITERARY CRITIC.

EVENING FALLS AND I START CRAWLING UP THE WALLS. MY FATHER THROWS AN APPLE AT ME IN DISGUST AND REMOVES MY BEDROOM FURNITURE.

I CANNOT SLEEP AND I CANNOT DREAM, I CAN'T EVEN SUPPORT A FAMILY OR TAKE A HOLIDAY TO BAVARIA AND MY BACK ACHES AND I DECIDE NOT TO DECIDE.

My Day by W. H. Auden

DECIDE WHAT YOU WANT OR OUGHT TO DO DURING THE DAY, THEN ALWAYS DO IT AT EXACTLY THE SAME MOMENT EVERYDAY, AND PASSION WILL GIVE YOU NO TROUBLE.

6:30 A.M. I AWAKEN. THE SUREST WAY TO DISCIPLINE PASSION IS TO DISCIPLINE TIME.

BENZEDRINE

6:33 A.M. A LITTLE SOMETHING TO LIFT MY SPIRITS, ON SCHEDULE. I'M A NEUROTIC MIDDLE-AGED BUTTERBALL KEPT TOGETHER BY MY REGULAR HABITS...

AND THAT GAME OF KNOWLEDGE, THAT BRINGING TO CONSCIOUSNESS, BY NAMING THEM, OF EMOTIONS AND THEIR HIDDEN RELATIONSHIPS, CALLED POETRY.

HAVE YOU GOT SOME SPARE CASH WYSTAN, I WANT TO BUY BAGELS FOR BREAKFAST.

WILL THIS BE ENOUGH CHESTER?

MISS GOD HAS DECIDED THAT I AM TO BE A WRITER, BUT HAVE NO OTHER FUN, AND NO TALENT FOR MAKING OTHERS AS HAPPY AS I WOULD LIKE THEM TO BE.

LATER...

WHEN WILL YOU BE HOME?

THE IDEAL AUDIENCE THE POET IMAGINES CONSISTS OF THE BEAUTIFUL WHO GO TO BED WITH HIM THE POWERFUL WHO INVITE HIM TO DINNER AND TELL HIM SECRETS OF STATE, AND HIS FELLOW POETS.

THE AUDIENCE HE GETS CONSISTS OF MYOPIC SCHOOLMASTERS, PIMPLY YOUNG MEN WHO EAT IN CAFETERIAS, AND HIS FELLOW POETS. SO ONE WRITES FOR ONE'S FELLOW POETS.

10 A.M. HOLY COMMUNION. THE SERIOUS PART OF PRAYER BEGINS WHEN WE HAVE GOT OUR BEGGING OVER WITH.

THERE'S AN IDIOTIC TUNE IN MY SOUP.

12 P.M. LUNCHTIME ACCORDING TO SCHEDULE. I EAT AN ENORMOUS AMOUNT IN A CAFETERIA BUT AM FORCED TO FOREGO DESSERT.

POETS ARE TOUGH AND CAN PROFIT FROM THE MOST DREADFUL EXPERIENCES

1:56 P.M. HOME AGAIN. CHESTER STILL OUT. HE MAKES ME SUFFER AND COMMIT FOLLIES WITHOUT WHICH I SHOULD SOON BECOME LIKE THE LATER TENNYSON.

U.S. MAIL

I SEND SOME MANUSCRIPTS TO MRS. DODDS IN ENGLAND, ASKING HER TO SIT ON THE LOUSY ONES - AND ASK OXFORD UNIVERSITY PRESS TO SEND MONEY,

THIS GIRL IS INVULNERABLE TO ALL BUT ONE, YOU OLD BRUNHILDE!

THEN INDULGE IN WAGNER AT THE MET. OPERA IS MY CHIEF LUXURY. I MISS CHRISTOPHER ISHERWOOD, WHO SHOULD NOT BE IN HOLLYWOOD... AND CHESTER.

I'VE NEVER ENOUGH BLANKETS

I READ A BIT. I BITE MY NAILS. MY FEET POINT TO THE RISING MOON.

My Day by Walt Whitman

10 A.M. MY SOUL AND I AWAKEN ON THIS FIRST DAY. I ENJOY THE ECSTASY OF SIMPLE PHYSIOLOGICAL BEING,

SIX OYSTERS AND TWO BUCKWHEAT CAKES. THE MAIL BRINGS FIVE LOVE MISSIVES FROM FEMALE ADMIRERS. I ENVY OTHER MEN THEIR CHILDREN, NEVER THEIR WIVES.

THE SUBTLE ELECTRIC FIRE THAT FOR YOUR SAKE IS PLAYING WITHIN ME...

THE SOUL OF THE MAN I SPEAK FOR REJOICES ONLY IN COMRADES.

I'LL OPEN THE SHUTTERS WHEN THE METHODIST CHURCH BELLS STOP!

ARE YOU ALLRIGHT IN THERE WALT?

I BURN SOME OLD PAPERS TOO SACRED, TOO SURLY AND ONLY MINE TO BE PERPETUATED. I HAVE TWICE DESTROYED A MASS OF LETTERS TO BE READY FOR WHAT MIGHT HAPPEN.

SO LONG WALT!

WHY READ MARK TWAIN?

I NOURISH THE REAL ME WITH A WALK BY THE RIVER. I GET MORE REAL FUN TALKING TO THE BOAT MEN FOR HALF AN HOUR THAN FROM ALL THE BOOKS BY ALL THE AMERICAN HUMOURISTS.

THE DIRTIEST BOOK IS THE EXPURGATED BOOK...

2 P.M. LUNCH WITH R.W. EMERSON WHO THINKS I SHOULD CUT SEX OUT OF MY NEXT EDITION OF "LEAVES OF GRASS". IF I CUT SEX OUT I MIGHT AS WELL CUT EVERYTHING OUT. RALPH PAYS. I AM PENNILESS. NOBODY WANTS TO HIRE A KOSMOS, EVEN THOUGH I HAVE A LETTER FROM RALPH.

I LOOK THROUGH AN OLD EGYPTOLOGY CATALOGUE. I AM REMINDED OF MY CAREER. THE PUBLIC IS A THICK-SKINNED BEAST... YOU HAVE TO KEEP WHACKING AWAY AT ITS HIDE TO LET IT KNOW YOU ARE THERE.

I ADD EIGHT POEMS TO MY NEW EDITION OF "LEAVES OF GRASS", AND WRITE TWO REVIEWS (FAVOURABLE) OF THE NEW EDITION FOR THE PAPERS.

WHEN SHALL I MAKE THE IDIOMATIC BOOK FOR MY LAND? OR A BIBLE FOR THE AMERICAN CHURCH?!

THE UNITED STATES THEMSELVES ARE ESSENTIALLY THE GREATEST POEM!

OOOOAAAH

PLINK!

PLINK!

BUT ALL WORDS ARE MEAN BEFORE THE LANGUAGE OF TRUE MUSIC. THE GUM IS WASHED FROM ONE'S EYE! THE PERFECT WRITER WOULD MAKE WORDS SING, DANCE, BEAR CHILDREN!

10 P.M. I DREAM IN MY DREAM ALL THE DREAMS OF THE OTHER DREAMERS, AND I BECOME THE OTHER DREAMERS.

My Day by Henry Miller

7 A.M. EVERY FACET OF ME AWAKENS: THE SENSUAL ME, THE PHILOSOPHICAL ME, THE RELIGIOUS ME, THE AESTHETIC ME.

I STRUGGLE TO GET OUT WHAT'S BELOW, IN THE SOLAR PLEXUS, IN THE NETHER REGIONS,

BUT I CAN ONLY WRITE AS MUCH TRUTH AS MY EGO PERMITS.

MIDDAY. THE HOUR I WAS BORN, MY ASTROLOGICAL PEAK. I'M WRITING LIKE AN ANGEL, IT'S COMING OUT LIKE WATER FROM A FAUCET — WHEN I AM RUDELY INTERRUPTED.

SEVEN YEARS WITH THIS VOICE LIKE PEA SOUP. IT'S ABOUT TIME FOR A DIVORCE. I TRY TO KEEP FRESH.

I COFFEE OUT. A GERMAN MOUTH. FRENCH EARS. RUSSIAN ARSE. CUNT INTERNATIONAL.

OF COURSE, ATTACHED TO THE WOMAN'S CUNT IS ALWAYS THE WOMAN HERSELF, AN EXCELLENT PING PONG PLAYER.

I PLAY A STEADY, DEFENSIVE, ZEN-LIKE GAME. IT IS MY CHINESE NATURE.

DING DONG. IT'S NOT A TELEGRAM FROM WESTERN UNION, BUT A GIFT FROM ONE OF MY BENEFACTRESSES.

FOR ME IT IS NO PROBLEM TO DEPEND ON OTHERS. BY LETTING PEOPLE HELP YOU, YOU DO THEM A SERVICE. YOU AID THEM TO BECOME BIGGER, MORE GENEROUS, MORE MAGNANIMOUS.

6 P.M. I DON'T FEEL LIKE COCKTAILS. I REWRITE THE TROPIC OF CANCER INSTEAD.

I CAN'T SLEEP. I WRITE ABOUT MYSELF. I COULD GO ON FOREVER.

My Day by Isaac Newton

6 A.M. I DO NOT AWAKEN, I HAVE NOT BEEN TO SLEEP.

I MISSED EVENING CHAPEL LAST EVENING. I THINK I WILL MISS MORNING CHAPEL. I WILL GO ON SUNDAY.

WHICH BRINGS ME TO MY HYPOTHESIS OF COLOURS. I CANNOT DEMONSTRATE IT FOR WANT OF ANOTHER PRISM. I WILL HAVE TO WAIT A YEAR TO PURCHASE ONE AT THE NEXT STURBRIDGE FAIR.

WHICH MAY NOT HOLD ME UP IN THE LEAST. THE SUN DOESN'T SHINE IN CAMBRIDGE EVERY DAY.

I GRIND A LENS FOR MY REFLECTING TELESCOPE, INSTEAD. I HAVE UNFORTUNATELY MADE ITS INVENTION A MATTER OF PUBLIC KNOWLEDGE.

I HAVE BEEN INUNDATED WITH LETTERS EVER SINCE, WHICH I MUST ANSWER, AND SACRIFICED MY PEACE, A MATTER OF REAL SUBSTANCE.

I DEFINE THE CONCEPT OF THE DIAMETRICAL HYPERBOLE AND SUFFER A COUGHING FIT. I TREAT IT WITH LUCATELLO BALSAM.

TRINITY COLLEGE IS SO EMPTY SINCE PLAGUE. I CUT MY MATHEMATICS LECTURE SHORT TO FIFTEEN MINUTES AS THERE ARE NO STUDENTS IN ATTENDANCE.

I THINK IT IS DINNER TIME. AT LEAST OTHERS SEEM TO BE EATING.

I DON'T KNOW WHY I MISSED DINNER. NO MATTER, TWO FRIENDS HAVE DECIDED TO VISIT ME IN MY CHAMBERS.

I THINK I'LL GET THEM SOME WINE... BUT REALLY THE ENDEAVOURS OF RECEDING FROM THE SUN WILL BE RECIPROCALLY AS THE SQUARES FROM...

AND THE ENDEAVOUR OF THE MOON TO RECEDE FROM THE CENTRE OF THE EARTH CAN BE COMPARED WITH...

My Day by Marcel Duchamp

9 A.M. A BELL.

ROSITA, THE NEW SPANISH MAID, BRINGS ME BREAKFAST IN BED.

MY CAFE AU LAIT IS COLD, DESPITE THE FUR CUP.

I THINK I'LL FINISH MY NUDE DESCENDING THE STAIRCASE TOMORROW.

I COULD CARVE SOME MARBLE SUGAR CUBES FOR MY NEXT PROJECT, IT'S GOOD THERAPY, BUT I'D MUCH RATHER A GAME OF CHESS.

I KNOW! I COULD GO AND CHECK THE DUST ON THE GREAT GLASS. IT HAS BEEN COLLECTING NEW YORK DUST FOR TWO AND A HALF YEARS... AND THEN PLAY CHESS

OH MON DIEU! IS THIS WHAT I GET FOR HIRING A SPANISH MAID?

READY FOR EXHEEBEETION!

TWO YEARS' WORK DOWN THE DRAIN. I'LL HAVE TO GO BACK TO SIMPLER WORKS, LIKE MY FOUNTAIN.

SALUT MARCEL!

BUT AN UNEXPECTED VISITOR TAKES ME FROM MY TROUBLES. HELLO MAN RAY.

AT LAST I GET DOWN TO SOMETHING REALLY IMPORTANT AND CHALLENGING.

WHO NEEDS ART WHEN YOU CAN PLAY CHESS?!

6 A.M. I AWAKEN, NOT AT BALMORAL, FORTUNATELY.

CHARLES IS NOT HIMSELF,

AND THEN HE IS.

I SIFT THROUGH THIS MORNING'S CORRESPONDENCE.

I JUST MISS PRINCESS ANNE. WHO'S BROUGHT WILLIAM A GIFT FROM THE HEART. PITY.

I DON'T FEEL LIKE SHOPPING TODAY, SOMEHOW. I FEEL LIKE OPAL FRUITS, MALTESERS, FRUIT GUMS AND A BIG MAC, IN THAT ORDER,

BUT SETTLE FOR WINDSOR'S NO-FRILLS DIET FARE: GAME GELEE FROM SANDRINGHAM AND CHEESE FROM THE ROYAL JERSEY HERD.

WILL'S UPSET. HE'S NOT BEEN THE SAME SINCE MARGARET THATCHER SENT HIM THAT MOBILE HE CAN NEVER QUITE REACH.

BUT I CAN'T STAY. I HAVE TO INAUGURATE SOMETHING (AGAIN).

WILL'S JUST SETTLING DOWN WHEN CHARLES MENTIONS HAVING LORD AND LADY TRY-ON TO DINNER THURSDAY. MAYBE NEXT YEAR.

7 P.M. WILL I WEAR THE DUCK-EGG SAPPHIRE BROOCH, THE SUNRAY DIAMOND NECKLACE, THE EMERALD CHOKER, THE SIX-STRAND PEARL CHOKER OR THE FEATHER BROOCH TO SEE "E.T."?

BEDTIME. CHARLES IS HIMSELF. HE ALWAYS IS.

My Day by Aubrey Beardsley

10:30 A.M. – I AM WOKEN BY MY SISTER AND MAMA.

11:05 – THE POSTMAN ARRIVES WITH A LETTER OF ENCOURAGEMENT FROM BURNE-JONES AND ONE OF DISCOURAGEMENT FROM BOSIE DOUGLAS.

I HAVE SEVEN DISTINCT STYLES, AND HAVE WON SUCCESS IN ALL OF THEM. MY PUBLISHER THINKS OTHERWISE!

I WITHDRAW THE "OBSCENE" ILLUSTRATION IN QUESTION, AND SUPPLY IN ITS PLACE A NEW ONE, SIMPLY BEAUTIFUL AND QUITE IRRELEVANT.

"UNCLEANLINESS IS NEXT TO BODLINESS!" PUNCH DOESN'T LIKE THE YELLOW BOOK EITHER.

I TAKE REFUGE AT THE CAFÉ ROYAL, BUT RUN INTO OSCAR WILDE INSTEAD. HE SAYS I'M AFFECTED.

REALLY I BELIEVE I'M SO AFFECTED EVEN MY LUNGS ARE AFFECTED.

I LEFT THE TASSEL OFF MY CANE AND CAUGHT A COLD. I HOPE MAMA DOESN'T PACK ME OFF TO BORNEMOUTH FOR A REST CURE. I SO MISS LONDON,

MY SISTER AND OUR AMATEUR THEATRICALS.

I FALL ASLEEP AT THE DINNER TABLE.

BUT I AM NOT DEAD. I MAKE IT TO THE OPERA.

AND TO WORK, WHEN IT IS LATE ENOUGH AND DARK ENOUGH TO SUMMON THE MUSES.

My Day by Nellie Melba

7:03 A.M. I AWAKEN TO YET ANOTHER INDIFFERENT BREAKFAST AT THE SAVOY. MR. ESCOFFIER MUST BE ON HOLIDAYS.

I SHOULD PREFER TO STAY IN MY OWN HOME, BUT I MUST GIVE MY FRENCH CRAFTSMEN TIME IF I WANT GREAT CUMBERLAND PALACE TO REALLY LOOK LIKE VERSAILLES.

11 A.M. MY LARYNGOLOGIST SEES TO MY NOSE AND THROAT. WE TAKE TEA AFTER THE CONSULTATION.

I COULD NOT DO COVENT GARDEN WITHOUT HIM. WHEN YOU ARE THE DIVA YOU HAVE TO BE THE BEST, ALWAYS!

I HAVE LUNCH WITH MY FRIEND AND PATRONESS LADY DE GREY, AND WE DECIDE WHO WILL NOT MAKE COVENT GARDEN THIS YEAR...

OR THE NEXT. WE ARE ADDING THE FINAL TOUCH TO OUR MEAL WITH SOME "FRAISES MELBA", WHEN ALFRED DE ROTHCHILD RINGS TO ASK ME TO TEA.

ALFRED GIVES ME CAKES AND FINANCIAL ADVICE AND ASKS WHEN WE ARE GOING TO HEAR SOME MORE WAGNER. I REMIND HIM OF HIS SNORING THROUGH VALKYRIE.

BACK AT MY HOTEL I CONTINUE TO THINK ABOUT WAGNER. WHY CAN I NOT DO JUSTICE TO HIM (ESPECIALLY WHEN IT IS THE FASHION)?

I THINK OF MY BELOVED DUKE OF ORLEANS FAR AWAY ON SAFARI IN AFRICA, WHEN AN ORCHID POKES THROUGH MY DOOR.

IT IS MY WONDERFUL FRIEND HERMANN BEMBERG WHO HAS COME TO TAKE ME TO THE THEATRE. I REMEMBER WHO THE DIVA IS!

I AM SINGING WITH CARUSO, WHO REPLACES MY CHEWING GUM WITH CHEWING TOBACCO BETWEEN ACTS,

WHICH IS POSSIBLY WHY I INSIST HE BE PAID £1 LESS THAN I PER PERFORMANCE, THOUGH NOT ENTIRELY. THERE IS ONLY ONE MELBA.

My Day by Albert Camus

7:30 A.M. NOT TURKISH COFFEE AGAIN.

I AM LATE FOR SOCCER PRACTICE. I HOP A BUS.

MY FACE SCREWED UP, MY SHOULDERS TIGHT, I BEGIN TO PLAY...

RUNNING HARD, MY FOOT FINALLY TOUCHES THE DUST-COVERED MASS.

IT FLIES TOWARD THE GOAL THROUGH THE HOT ALGERIAN AIR,

AND IS CAUGHT BY THE OPPOSITE TEAM'S GOAL-KEEPER.

I GO DOWN AGAIN TO THE CENTRE OF THE FIELD, AND MAKE A FRESH START, WITH ARMS OUT-STRETCHED.

AS I PERSPIRE IN THE HOT ALGERIAN AIR AND THE BALL SOARS TOWARD THE GOAL, I REALIZE THAT THE BALL IS MY THING,

EVEN WHEN IT IS CAUGHT BY THE OPPOSITE TEAM'S GOALKEEPER (AGAIN)

WITH THE HOLY HUMAN SECURITY OF TWO DUST CLOTTED FEET, I MAKE A FRESH START WITH ARMS OUTSTRETCHED (AGAIN).

IT IS DURING THIS RE-TURN, THIS PAUSE, THAT I REALIZE MY FATE BELONGS TO ME...

AND ALL IS ..... WELL ...

My Day by Rip Van Winkle

DAWN – I DO NOT AWAKEN, AGAIN.

I DO NOT BREAKFAST.

I ANSWER NO PHONE CALLS.

A LADY WHOM I DO NOT KNOW BY THE NAME OF EDELMIRA CALLS;

BUT I AM OUT TO LUNCH,

AND AFTERNOON TEA,

UNFORTUNATELY.

I SKIP A GAME OF TWILIGHT TENNIS.

7 P.M. AND IT'S TIME FOR COCKTAILS.

BUT I DON'T HAVE THE FIXINGS FOR A MARGARITA.

I FANCY A HOLIDAY IN ACAPULCO.

TOMORROW, MAYBE.

My Day by Hernán Cortés

TENOCHTITLÁN 8 A.M. DOÑA MARINA BRINGS ME SOME HOT COCOA AND GUACAMOLE.

THE DOÑA AND I ARE OFF TO MASS IN THE TEOCALLI. WE BID THE EMPEROR JOIN US, BUT HE DECLINES.

IT MIGHT HAVE DONE HIM GOOD TO GET OUT OF THE PALACE. EVER SINCE WE TOOK HIM PRISONER HE HAS BECOME QUITE DESPONDENT,

AND WILL NOT LISTEN TO ANYBODY.

I HAD ARRANGED FOR THE TEOCALLI TO BE TIDIED UP FOR MASS BUT IT IS NOT READY AND WE HAVE TO WAIT.

IN THE MEANTIME, WITH THE HELP OF THE DOÑA, I PICK UP SOME NICE BITS AND PIECES FOR THE FOLKS BACK IN EXTREMADURA.

WE RETURN TO THE PALACE. ONLY THREE INDIAN CONVERTS TODAY. I WILL HAVE TO DO SOMETHING MORE POSITIVE TOWARD THE CONQUEST OF MEXICO NEXT WEEK.

I FIND THE EMPEROR MONTEZUMA GIVING AWAY JEWELLERY TO AN ARQUEBUSIER. HE IS REALLY QUITE BORED,

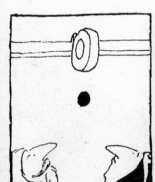

SO I CHALLENGE HIM TO A GAME OF TOTOLOQUE.

QUITE EXHAUSTED, WE RETIRE TO SOME READING. IT IS NORMALLY AT THIS TIME THAT I HAVE MY LESSON IN NAHUATL, BUT DOÑA MARINA IS COMPLAINING OF A BACKACHE.

AS I RETIRE I WONDER WHAT BROUGHT ME TO THESE FARAWAY SHORES, AND THEN I REMEMBER.

BUT IT DOES LITTLE TO CURE MY HOMESICKNESS. I WILL HAVE TO DO SOMETHING ABOUT THOSE PYRAMIDS ON MONDAY.

My Day by Dylan Thomas

6 A.M. I FINALLY GET TO SLEEP, BUT IT'S TIME TO WAKE UP.

MY WIFE CAITLIN ENQUIRES AFTER MY LATEST FILM SCRIPT. IT IS LATE AS USUAL AND SHE SUGGESTS I STICK TO POETRY.

SHE INSISTS IN FACT. (CAITLIN IS IRISH)

BUT I DIDN'T BORROW THIS FANCY COAT FROM CONSTANTINE FITZGIBBON, NOR THIS BERET FROM GRAHAM GREENE, NOR THIS CRAVAT FROM ONE OF EDITH SITWELL'S HOUSEGUESTS FOR NOTHING.

SO I GET BACK TO WORK BUT FIND THAT I AM UNWELL AND UNABLE TO CONCENTRATE.

I REMEMBER MY DIABETIC DOCTOR'S PROPHECY — THAT I WILL DIE IN THREE YEARS — AND GO OUT FOR A PINT.

I MEET SOME AMERICAN TOURISTS AND TELL THEM I AM A PROFESSOR OF LINGUISTIC PHILOSOPHY AT THE UNIVERSITY OF PATAGONIA ON SABBATICAL LEAVE. THEY BUY ME ANOTHER PINT.

I ARRIVE HOME TO FIND MY AGENT WHO HAS DROPPED IN FROM LONDON. HE SUGGESTS THAT I STOP WRITING CHEQUES AND EATING. (HE ALSO LENDS ME HIS LOVELY TIEPIN).

I START WORKING ON AN AMERICAN TRAVELOGUE THE PUBLISHER IS BOUND TO GIVE ME QUITE A BIT FOR. PERHAPS I WOULD BE BETTER OFF PULLING TEETH.

BUT CAITLIN AND I HAVE BEEN ASKED OUT TO DINNER. I WILL THINK ABOUT HONEY TOMORROW.

DINNER WAS SUPERB BUT CAITLIN INSISTS ON DANCING FOR THE GUESTS.

WE WALK HOME. CAITLIN IS NOT AT ALL PLEASED THAT I HAVE WALKED OUT WITH OUR FRIENDS' PERSIAN CARPET. BUT IF SHE CAN DANCE, I CAN BORROW. IN ANY CASE IT WILL LOOK NICE IN THE LIVING ROOM.

My Day by Dame Edna May Everage

9 A.M.– I, MY GOOD SELF, AWAKEN. I'M BACK IN MELBOURNE IN TIME (HOPEFULLY) FOR THE AUSTRALIAN CULTURAL RENAISSANCE.

9:30 A.M. IF MY DAUGHTER VALMAI COULD SEE ME NOW, POSSUMS. THIS IS A LOT EASIER OF COURSE IF YOU ARE A TINTED PERSON.

IN THE WORDS OF SOME POOR COUNTRY PERSON, POSSUMS, "LIFE WASN'T MEANT TO BE EASY." I'M OUT OF MUESLI. I SOAK SOME OF VALMAI'S PASSIONFRUIT CRUNCHIES INSTEAD.

10:03–11:34 A.M. I WASH. I LOOK FORWARD TO COMING HOME TO AUSTRALIA TO WASH, BLOSSOMS, SOMETHING THAT IS NOT ALWAYS DONE IN OTHER COUNTRIES WITH A REGULARITY.

12:01 P.M. HAVING PUT MY VICTORIAN VEGGIE SHAPE IN THE FRIDGE FOR LUNCH, I SETTLE DOWN TO SOME LIGHT READING, A HABIT I MY GOOD SELF, DEVELOPED EARLIER IN LIFE.

I SHOULD REALLY PAY A VISIT TO MY HUSBAND NORM IN HOZZIE, BUT I CAN'T GO TOO OFTEN – CAN'T HAVE HIM BECOMING A SPECIALLY PAMPERED INVALID!

MY VEGGIE SHAPE IS JUST THE RIGHT CONSISTENCY, AND SO CHEAP TO COOK UP, MUMS – EVEN PAUPERS CAN AFFORD ONE, USING A SMALLER MOULD.

I'M OFF FOR MY DAILY CONSTITUTIONAL THROUGH GREATER MELBOURNE IN SEARCH OF GLADS FOR MY SHOW WHEN I RUN INTO MY OLD BRIDESMAID, MADGE ALLSOP.

MADGE IS ALL ARMADILLO ELBOWS AND SUPERFLUOUS HAIR, A PILLAR OF AUSTRALIAN NEGLECT, POSSUMS.

7:43 P.M. I PREPARE FOR MY SHOW. I'M DOUBLE-BILLED WITH BARRY HUMPHRIES.

THE OLD POSSUM'S STILL HANGING ON AT HIS AGE. POOR BLOSSOM. WHEN WILL HE EVER LEARN?

My Day by Jorge Luis Borges

6 A.M.— I AM LOST IN A LABYRINTH. STILL, A NIGHTMARE IS BETTER THAN INSOMNIA.

OR IS IT? I AWAKEN TO FIND MYSELF A VICTIM OF THE DECIMAL SYSTEM. ACCORDING TO IT I AM IN MY EIGHTIES.

IF WE COUNTED EVERY TWELVE OR FOURTEEN YEARS I WOULD ONLY BE SIXTY.

MAYBE I'LL GET THE NOBEL PRIZE NEXT YEAR. MY FAME IS ENOUGH TO CONDEMN THIS AGE.

OVER LUNCH I AM REMINDED OF AMERICANS. AMERICANS DON'T THINK ABOUT GOOD FOOD, THEY THINK ABOUT VITAMINS AND MINERALS.

THE ENGLISH ARE NOT MUCH BETTER, THEY HAVE FILLED THE WORLD WITH STUPIDITIES LIKE SOCCER.

BLISS. A CUP OF COLOMBIAN COFFEE. IN MY YOUTH I TRIED MESCALIN AND COCAINE BUT I SWITCHED IMMEDIATELY TO PEPPERMINTS WHICH I FOUND MORE STIMULATING.

AN AFTERNOON WALK— FROM PARADISE TO HELL, FROM HELL TO PURGATORY, FROM PURGATORY TO LIMBO, FROM LIMBO TO PARADISE, AND PARADISE AGAIN TO HELL.

6 P.M. AT THE SOCIETY OF CRIME NOVEL WRITERS. I GIVE OUT THE PRIZE FOR BEST HARDBACK AND BEST PAPERBACK. PRIZES FOR THE PAPER, NOT THE TEXT! (?)

I CONSIDER DEMOCRACY TO BE AN ABUSE OF STATISTICS

I HATE GROUP SPORTS LIKE SOCCER AND COCKTAILS.

I AM NOT CERTAIN OF BEING A CHRISTIAN, I AM CERTAIN OF NOT BEING A BUDDHIST, BUT A BAD TOOTHACHE IS ENOUGH TO DENY THE EXISTENCE OF AN ALL-POWERFUL GOD.

I'D FEEL BETTER, IF I COULD GET RID OF MY TEETH OR BE SURE (') WRITTEN ONE GOOD STORY OR POEM. GOODNIGHT.

My Day by Vincent van Gogh

7 A.M.- I AWAKEN

WE BREAKFAST IN. GAUGUIN SAYS IT'S CHEAPER THAT WAY. I THINK I'M DEPRESSED.

SO IS EVERYBODY ELSE.

I PAINT SIX VASES WITH FOURTEEN SUNFLOWERS TO BRIGHTEN UP MY STUDIO.

LUNCHTIME. WE EAT IN. GAUGUIN SAYS IT'S CHEAPER THAT WAY. THEO IS LATE WITH MY ALLOWANCE AGAIN.

I WRITE TO THEO.

GAUGUIN GOES "OUT". TOO MUCH OF IT WEAKENS THE BRAIN YOU KNOW— POOR PAUL.

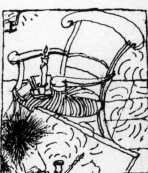

I PAINT HIS CHAIR.

HIDEOUS WIND AND THEN RAIN. MY WINTER DEPRESSION BEGINS, AND IT'S ONLY SEPTEMBER. SO MUCH FOR MOVING TO THE SOUTH OF FRANCE.

ABSINTH WARMS THE COCKLES OF MY HEART,

AND I DISCOVER THE NIGHT— MORE BEAUTIFUL, MORE RICHLY COLOURED THAN THE DAY!

PAUL IS STILL OUT. I PAINT MY CHAIR. GOODNIGHT.

My Day by Ronald Reagan

7:05 A.M. - A STAR IS BORNE. I AWAKEN IN TIME TO MAKE AMERICA GREAT AGAIN!

HOLY TOLEDO! WHERE'S THE REST OF ME?

IT'S O.K., NOW I AM NOT JUST A THREAT TO ERROL FLYNN.

SHOOT! MY BULLET-PROOF VEST REALLY DOES MAKE ME LOOK FAT.

MOVE OVER JANE FONDA! I WORK OUT. I BUILT A 400 FOOT FENCE OUT OF TELEPHONE POLES LAST SUMMER.

THAT WAS BETWEEN MEMOS. I HATE MEMOS. I HAVE THEM STAMPED "DECISION" OR "INFORMATION" SO THAT THERE IS NO CONFUSION OVER WHAT HAS TO BE DONE.

I SKIP FOREIGN POLICY. ONE WAY TO HELP BUDGET DEFICITS WOULD BE BY EVERYONE LIVING UP TO THE TEN COMMANDMENTS AND OBEYING THE GOLDEN RULE.

MEANWHILE IN RODEO DRIVE

GUCC

I'M HUNGRY— WHERE'S "MOMMY*"? PROBABLY IN SACRAMENTO AMIDST THE CYPRESSES AND GINKO TREES.

*NANCY REAGAN.

I HAVE A LUNCHEON ANYWAY. I ADDRESS "THOSE ON MY RIGHT" AND THOSE "ON THE AUDIENCE'S RIGHT". I WOULDN'T WANT TO EMBARRASS ANYONE BY SUGGESTING THEY'RE ON THE LEFT.

IF SOMEONE IS SETTING FIRE TO THE HOUSE IT DOESN'T MATTER IF HE IS A DELIBERATE ARSONIST OR JUST A FOOL PLAYING WITH MATCHES. THE RESULT WILL BE THE SAME.

MY HUSBAND DOESN'T MAKE SNAP DECISIONS, BUT DOESN'T OVERTHINK EITHER!

IT'S NOT FIVE O'CLOCK YET. TALLY HO! THERE'S NO BETTER TIME TO MAKE A DECISION THAN WHEN IT'S RIGHT IN FRONT OF YOU.

THE END

9 P.M. AT LAST! IT'S FINALLY BEDTIME FOR BONZO. TOODLE-OOO!